简明语音教程

主编　岳丽鸽
编委　安　邦　　陈　冰　　关　峥
　　　李婷婷　　李伟娟　　李　莹
　　　刘　珺　　孙超然　　仵茹楠
　　　杨　静

河南大学出版社
HENAN UNIVERSITY PRESS
郑州

图书在版编目(CIP)数据

简明语音教程/岳丽鸽主编. -- 郑州:河南大学出版社,2024.7. -- ISBN 978-7-5649-6003-2

Ⅰ.G634.411

中国国家版本馆 CIP 数据核字第 2024KR8912 号

责任编辑　屈琳玉
责任校对　林方丽
封面设计　马　龙

出　版	河南大学出版社		
	地址:郑州市郑东新区商务外环中华大厦 2401 号	邮编:450046	
	电话:0371-22864494(基础教育出版分社)		
	0371-86059701(营销部)	网址:hupress.henu.edu.cn	
排　版	郑州市今日文教印制有限公司		
印　刷	郑州豫兴印刷有限公司		
版　次	2024 年 8 月第 1 版	印　次	2024 年 8 月第 1 次印刷
开　本	787 mm×1092 mm　1/16	印　张	7.5
字　数	164 千字	定　价	22.00 元

(本书如有印装质量问题,请与河南大学出版社营销部联系调换。)

序

在《义务教育英语课程标准(2022年版)》背景下,义务教育阶段的英语教学正在经历着新一轮的改革和挑战。新课标对义务教育阶段的英语语音教学的要求更加明确细致,更加着眼于培养学生的终身学习能力。

在新课标视域下,为使初中英语教师在七年级起始阶段在开展英语语音教学时有所依托,提升初中小学英语语音衔接教学的效度,《简明语音教程》在中原名师岳丽鸽初中英语工作室的策划和努力下诞生了。

各校可根据学生生情和教师的英语语音教学实施能力,对此教程进行校本化的探索使用。

作者建议在七年级起始阶段,进行为期一个月的英语语音衔接教学,这一个月称为"英语语音素养突破月"。

通过语音衔接教学,期望达到以下目标:

第一,学生能完成48个国际音标的基本单音准确发音和规范书写;

第二,学生能够正确划分音节,根据音标自主读出任意单词,尤其是做到拼读重音无误;

第三,在英语学习中,当遇到生词时,学生能够学会使用词典查找其语音及语义,并根据词典上的音标拼读出单词;

第四,学生能够正确、规范书写26个字母的大小写,并能够准确掌握26个字母的发音;

第五,学生能够掌握连读、失去爆破、句子中的重读单词和非重读单词等语音技能;

第六,学生能够在不同的句子类型和语境中使用正确的语调;

第七,学生能够了解英美音的差异,并在今后学习中不断规范自己的发音;

第八，学生能够在教师的指导下进行语流训练，做到有感情地、语音纯正地朗读英语对话和语篇。

第九，学生能够掌握自主学习英语生词的技能，在音节知识的辅助下提升单词的识记能力。

第十，学生可以在阅读英语文章时，根据所学语音知识拼读出生词，在朗读英文文本时不会出现不自信、中断朗读的现象。

作者所期望的这十条学习目标用一句话来概括就是：希望学生能在这一个月中掌握英语语言学习的基本语音知识和语音技能，为其后期训练良好的英语语音语调打下坚实的理论基础和技能根基。

在进行语音教学的同时，作者亦希望英语教师能从"英语语音素养突破月"开始着手培养学生的英语背诵能力、英语书写能力和英语阅读能力。从最简单的字母、单词和英语文段开始，在学科知识相互融合的理念指引下，科学执教，引导和帮助学生培养良好的英语学习习惯和掌握科学的英语学习方法。

岳丽鸽

2024 年 6 月

目 录

Lesson 1　Monophthongs 单元音 …………………………………（ 1 ）

Lesson 2　Diphthongs 双元音 ……………………………………（ 10 ）

Lesson 3　Consonants Ⅰ 辅音(一) ………………………………（ 15 ）

Lesson 4　Consonants Ⅱ 辅音(二) ………………………………（ 24 ）

Lesson 5　Mixed practice of vowels and consonants 元音辅音混合练习

………………………………………………………………（ 33 ）

Lesson 6　Practice of monosyllables 单音节拼读练习 …………（ 42 ）

Lesson 7　Practice of disyllables 双音节拼读练习 ………………（ 47 ）

Lesson 8　Practice of polysyllables 多音节拼读练习 ……………（ 55 ）

Lesson 9　Mixed practice of monosyllables, disyllables and polysyllables

单音节、双音节、多音节混合拼读练习 ………………（ 60 ）

Lesson 10　Stress, liaison and loss of plosion 重读，连读，失去爆破

………………………………………………………………（ 64 ）

Lesson 11　Intonation of different types of sentences 不同类型的句子的

语调 ………………………………………………………（ 73 ）

Lesson 12　Review and examination of basic phonetic knowledge 基本

语音复习检测 ……………………………………………（ 84 ）

Lesson 13　Differences between British English and American English
　　　　　英式英语和美式英语区分 ························(88)

Lesson 14　Sentence imitation 句子模仿 ························(94)

Lesson 15　Dialogue imitation 对话模仿 ························(98)

Lesson 16　Passage imitation 语篇模仿 ························(102)

附表 1　英语国际音标四线三格书写规范 ························(104)

附表 2　26 个英文字母的书写及发音 ························(105)

附录 3　七年级新目标上册英语诵读小文 ························(106)

附录 4　《简明语音教程》使用参考手册 ························(112)

Lesson 1　Monophthongs 单元音

Ⅰ. [i:] Front vowel 前元音

1. Manner of articulation 发音要领

Make the mouth open and touch the lower front teeth lightly with the tip of your tongue. When this sound is made, keep smiling. It is produced with vocal cords vibration.

上下唇张开,舌尖轻抵下齿,嘴角尽量往两边拉伸,呈微笑状,振动声带。

2. Practice 发音练习

she [ʃi:]	we [wi:]	week [wi:k]	see [si:]	three [θri:]
thief [θi:f]	piece [pi:s]	ski [ski:]	eat [i:t]	key [ki:]

Ⅱ. [ɪ] Front vowel 前元音

1. Manner of articulation 发音要领

Compared with [i:], this sound should be short and fast, then make lips flat and touch the lower front teeth lightly with the tip of the tongue. It is produced with vocal cords vibration.

发音要短促而轻快,嘴唇两旁伸扁平,舌尖轻抵下齿,开口比 [i:] 大。需要振动声带。

2. Practice 发音练习

sit [sɪt]   bit [bɪt]   did [dɪd]   his [hɪz]   middle [ˈmɪdl]
city [ˈsɪti]   busy [ˈbɪzi]   baby [ˈbeɪbi]   build [bɪld]   monkey [ˈmʌŋki]

Ⅲ. [e] Front vowel 前元音

1. Manner of articulation 发音要领

First, make the lips flat and touch the lower front teeth lightly with the tip of the tongue. Raise the front of the tongue and an index finger can be passed between the upper and lower teeth. This sound should be short and produced with vocal cords vibration.

口形稍扁,舌尖轻抵下齿,舌前部稍抬起,上下齿之间能容一个食指,发音短促,振动声带。

2. Practice 发音练习

get [get]   let [let]   pen [pen]   desk [desk]   tell [tel]
bed [bed]   head [hed]   bread [bred]   friend [frend]   many [ˈmeni]

Ⅳ. [æ] Front vowel 前元音

1. Manner of articulation 发音要领

First, make the lips flat and touch the lower front teeth lightly with the tip of your tongue. It should be short. Open the mouth bigger than the sound of [e]. It is produced with vocal cords vibration.

舌尖轻抵下齿,双唇向两边张开,气流短促,比[e]开口要大一些。需要振动声带。

2. Practice 发音练习

cat [kæt]   fat [fæt]   bag [bæg]   map [mæp]   dad [dæd]
salad ['sæləd]   glad [glæd]   thank [θæŋk]   black [blæk]   family ['fæməli]

V. [ɜː] Central vowel 中元音

1. Manner of articulation 发音要领

Put the tongue forward and up a little more to make the long vowel with vocal cords vibration.

舌部略微隆起,振动声带,发长音。

2. Practice 发音练习

bird [bɜːd]   third [θɜːd]   hurt [hɜːt]   fur [fɜː]   church [tʃɜːtʃ]
learn [lɜːn]   early ['ɜːli]   her [hɜː(r)]   serve [sɜːv]   journal ['dʒɜːnl]

VI. [ə] Central vowel 中元音

1. Manner of articulation 发音要领

Put the tongue forward and up a little more to make the very short vowel with vocal cords vibration.

舌部略微隆起,振动声带,发短音。

2. Practice 发音练习

sister ['sɪstə(r)]   paper ['peɪpə(r)]   doctor ['dɒktə(r)]   color ['kʌlə(r)]
dollar ['dɒlə(r)]   police [pə'liːs]   tonight [tə'naɪt]   famous ['feɪməs]
upon [ə'pɒn]   ago [ə'gəʊ]

VII. [ʌ] Central vowel 中元音

1. Manner of articulation 发音要领

Slightly raise the tongue and open the mouth a little (bigger than smiling). This sound is short with vocal cords vibration.

舌部略抬,上下唇微张(比微笑时口形略大),发音短促,振动声带。

2. Practice 发音练习

love [lʌv]   come [kʌm]   blood [blʌd]   luck [lʌk]   sun [sʌn]
cut [cʌt]   but [bʌt]   club [klʌb]   country ['kʌntri]   under ['ʌndə(r)]

VIII. [ɑː] Back vowel 后元音

1. Manner of articulation 发音要领

Slightly raise the tongue and then keep it normally in the mouth. [ɑː] is the back vowel. It is produced with vocal cords vibration.

舌部略抬,平放口中,后舌稍稍隆起,发声部位靠后,振动声带。

2. Practice 发音练习

art [ɑːt]   start [stɑːt]   park [pɑːk]   dark [dɑːk]   March [mɑːtʃ]
aunt [ɑːnt]   after ['ɑːftə(r)]   fast [fɑːst]   dance [dɑːns]   class [klɑːs]

Ⅸ. [ɔː] Back vowel 后元音

1. Manner of articulation 发音要领

Make the mouth open. The back of the tongue goes up a little more to make the long sound. The tip of the tongue moves away from the lower front teeth. When this sound is made, the lips should be round.

上下唇张大,舌后部微微抬起,舌尖离开下齿,双唇收圆突出,发长音。

2. Practice 发音练习

horse [hɔːs]　　short [ʃɔːt]　door [dɔː(r)] four [fɔː(r)] daughter[ˈdɔːtə(r)]
August [ˈɔːɡəst] warm [wɔːm] draw [drɔː]　bought[bɔːt] also [ˈɔːlsəʊ]

Ⅹ. [ɒ] Back vowel 后元音

1. Manner of articulation 发音要领

The back of the tongue goes up a little more, the lips should be rounded but not protruded, and make the short sound with vocal cords vibration.

后舌部微微抬起,双唇略圆,但不突出,振动声带,发短音。

2. Practice 发音练习

hot [hɒt]　　lot [lɒt]　　sock [sɒk]　　stop [stɒp]　　cross [krɒs]
cough [kɒf]　want[wɒnt] wash [wɒʃ]　watch[wɒtʃ]　what [wɒt]

XI. [uː] Back vowel 后元音

1. Manner of articulation 发音要领

When the sound is made, the tongue rises up and backs a little more. The lips should be round. It is the long vowel with vocal cords vibration.

舌后部抬起,双唇突出且收圆,振动声带,发长音。

2. Practice 发音练习

rule [ruːl]　　June [dʒuːn]　　shoe [ʃuː]　　school [skuːl]　　tooth [tuːθ]
soup [suːp]　　group [gruːp]　　flew [fluː]　　fruit [fruːt]　　blue [bluː]

XII. [ʊ] Back vowel 后元音

1. Manner of articulation 发音要领

When the sound is made, the back of the tongue goes up a little more. The lips should be pursed but not protruded. It is the short vowel with vocal cords vibration.

后舌抬高,嘴唇噘起(但不能过于突出),振动声带,发短音。

2. Practice 发音练习

book [bʊk]　　cook [kʊk]　　good [gʊd]　　woman [ˈwʊmən]　　wolf [wʊlf]
full [fʊl]　　put [pʊt]　　would [wʊd]　　could [kʊd]　　should [ʃʊd]

Lesson 1　第一课时 Homework

Ⅰ. 英语书法练习。

1. 按照英语国际音标四线三格书写格式抄写 [iː] [ɪ] [e] [æ] [ɜː] [ə]各 5 遍。
2. 抄写 26 个英文字母中 Aa－Gg 各 5 遍,注意书写笔顺和字母占格。

Ⅱ. 跟读模仿以下单词发音,按要求提交模仿作业。

she [ʃiː]　　　bee [biː]　　　tea [tiː]　　　niece [niːs]
pig [pɪg]　　　rainy [ˈreɪni]　　monkey [ˈmʌŋki]　begin [bɪˈgɪn]
bed [bed]　　bread [bred]　　head [hed]　　friend [frend]
cat [kæt]　　　bad [bæd]　　　sat [sæt]　　　thank [θæŋk]
earth [ɜːθ]　　her [hɜː(r)]　　sir [sɜː(r)]　　purple [ˈpɜːpl]
father [ˈfɑːðə(r)]　doctor [ˈdɒktə(r)]　banana [bəˈnɑːnə]　tomato [təˈmɑːtəʊ]

Ⅲ. 跟读模仿下列句子或对话,按要求提交模仿作业。

1. Tongue twisters:
   Jill wishes she had fish and chips for dinner.
   Pete's eating meat with cheese and peas.
   Pete and Jill drink tea with milk.
2. A dialogue:
   Nathan: Hi, Kim. Why are you so happy today?
   Kim: Because it's the 23rd of February.
   Nathan: And what's special about that date?

Kim: It's my birthday!

Nathan: Really! Happy birthday, Kim.

Kim: Thanks. I'm 13 today.

Nathan: Lucky you!

Kim: When is your birthday, Nathan?

Nathan: It's in September.

Kim: What date?

Nathan: The 13th. I think it's on a Tuesday this year.

Lesson 1　第二课时 Homework

Ⅰ. 英语书法练习。

1. 按照英语国际音标四线三格书写格式抄写[ʌ] [ɑː] [ɔː] [ɒ] [uː] [ʊ]各5遍。

2. 抄写26个英文字母中 Hh－Nn 各5遍,注意书写笔顺和字母占格。

Ⅱ. 跟读模仿以下单词发音,按要求提交模仿作业。

come [kʌm]	bus [bʌs]	duck [dʌk]	enough [ɪˈnʌf]
class [klɑːs]	party [ˈpɑːti]	aunt [ɑːnt]	heart [hɑːt]
horse [hɔːs]	door [dɔː(r)]	call [kɔːl]	draw [drɔː]
sock [sɒk]	hot [hɒt]	dog [dɒg]	watch [wɒtʃ]
wash [wɒʃ]	cough [kɒf]	zoo [zuː]	food [fuːd]
do [duː]	who [huː]	rule [ruːl]	June [dʒuːn]
look [lʊk]	push [pʊʃ]	could [kʊd]	should [ʃʊd]

Ⅲ. 跟读模仿下列对话，按要求提交模仿作业。

Zoey: So, have you got any hobbies at all, Ellie?

Ellie: Yes, actually. I really enjoy making model aeroplanes.

Zoey: Model aeroplanes? That sounds cool.

Ellie: It is. Do you want to see them?

Zoey: Yes, please!

Ellie: OK. Come on. They're upstairs in my bedroom.

(*Moments later*)

Ellie: And here are my planes. That's my favourite.

Zoey: Cool! Can I pick it up?

Ellie: OK, but be careful. No, please! Don't do that! They don't fly!

Zoey: Oh, that's right. OK. Sorry.

Mum: Ellie? What are you up to?

Ellie: Nothing, Mum. My friend Zoey's here. We're looking at my planes.

Mum: OK. But hurry up. Dinner's almost ready.

Ellie: OK, Mum. Look out, Zoey! It's very …

Zoey: Oh no. It's broken!

Ellie: Yes, I know!

Zoey: I'm really sorry, Ellie. And it's your favourite, too.

Ellie: That's OK. I know it's an accident. I'm sure I can fix it.

Lesson 2　Diphthongs 双元音

Ⅰ. [aɪ]

1. Manner of articulation 发音要领

Firstly pronounce the long sound [ɑ:]. Then pronounce the short sound [ɪ]. Then join the two sounds. Touch the lower front teeth lightly with the tip of the tongue.

先发[ɑ:]的音,然后再滑向[ɪ],舌尖轻抵下齿。

2. Practice 发音练习

tiger [ˈtaɪgə(r)]　　bike [baɪk]　　life [laɪf]　　high [haɪ]　　light [laɪt]

height [haɪt]　　either [ˈaɪðə(r)]　　style [staɪl]　　sky [skaɪ]　　die [daɪ]

Ⅱ. [eɪ]

1. Manner of articulation 发音要领

Firstly pronounce the sound [e] and then pronounce the sound [ɪ]. Then join the two sounds. The first part of the sound should be pronounced more clearly and longer.

舌头从[e]的位置滑向[ɪ]的位置,双唇稍扁,发第一个音时较为清楚、较长,第二个音发得较模糊、较短。

2. Practice 发音练习

name [neɪm]　cake [keɪk]　place [pleɪs]　eight [eɪt]　weight [weɪt]
great [greɪt]　break [breɪk]　play [pleɪ]　say [seɪ]　they [ðeɪ]

Ⅲ. [ɔɪ]

1. Manner of articulation 发音要领

Firstly pronounce the sound [ɒ] and then pronounce the sound [ɪ]. Then join the two sounds. The lips will be changed from round to flat. The first part of the sound should be spoken longer and stronger.

舌头从[ɒ]的位置滑向[ɪ]的位置，双唇由圆到扁，前音长而强，后音短而弱。

2. Practice 发音练习

boy [bɔɪ]　　toy [tɔɪ]　　soy [sɔɪ]　　enjoy [ɪnˈdʒɔɪ]　joyful [ˈdʒɔɪfʊl]
oil [ɔɪl]　　boil [bɔɪl]　join [dʒɔɪn]　noisy [ˈnɔɪzi]　voice [vɔɪs]

Ⅳ. [ɪə]

1. Manner of articulation 发音要领

Firstly pronounce the sound [ɪ] and then pronounce the sound [ə]. Then join the two sounds. Your mouth will be changed from small to slightly open.

舌头从[ɪ]的位置向[ə]的位置滑动，口形从小变为略开。

2. Practice 发音练习

hero [ˈhɪərəʊ]　series [ˈsɪəriːz]　ear [ɪə(r)]　dear [dɪə(r)]　idea [aɪˈdɪə]
real [rɪəl]　　beer [bɪə(r)]　　peer [pɪə(r)]　here [hɪə(r)]　fierce [fɪəs]

V. [eə]

1. Manner of articulation 发音要领

Firstly pronounce the sound [e] and then pronounce the sound [ə]. Then join the two sounds with the lips naturally open.

舌头从[e]的位置向[ə]的位置滑动,嘴唇自然张开。

2. Practice 发音练习

parent ['peərnt]	vary ['veəri]	fair [feə(r)]	hair [heə(r)]
pear [peə(r)]	wear [weə(r)]	care [keə(r)]	dare [deə(r)]
where [weə(r)]	there [ðeə(r)]		

VI. [ʊə]

1. Manner of articulation 发音要领

Firstly pronounce the sound [ʊ] and then pronounce the sound [ə]. Then join the two sounds. The lips will be changed from round to their normal shape.

舌头从[ʊ]的位置向[ə]的位置滑动,嘴唇从圆变为正常。

2. Practice 发音练习

sure [ʃʊə(r)]	pure [pjʊə(r)]	assure [əˈʃʊə(r)]	gourd [gʊəd]
poor [pʊə(r)]	boor [bʊə(r)]	tour [tʊə(r)]	detour [ˈdiːtʊə(r)]
casual [ˈkæʒʊəl]	unusual [ʌnˈjuːʒʊəl]		

Ⅶ. [aʊ]

1. Manner of articulation 发音要领

Firstly pronounce the sound [a] and then pronounce the sound [ʊ]. Then join the two sounds with the gradually rounded lips.

舌头从[a]的位置向[ʊ]的位置滑动,嘴唇逐渐突出。

2. Practice 发音练习

cow [kaʊ]	now [naʊ]	town [taʊn]	flower ['flaʊə(r)]
brown [braʊn]	mouth [maʊθ]	shout [ʃaʊt]	house [haʊs]
cloud [klaʊd]	south [saʊθ]		

Ⅷ. [əʊ]

1. Manner of articulation 发音要领

Firstly pronounce the sound [ə] and then pronounce the sound [ʊ]. Then join the two sounds with the gradually rounded lips.

舌头从[ə]的位置向[ʊ]的位置滑动,嘴唇从自然变为圆唇。

2. Practice 发音练习

note [nəʊt]	most [məʊst]	hope [həʊp]	boat [bəʊt]
coat [kəʊt]	soul [səʊl]	shoulder ['ʃəʊldə(r)]	blow [bləʊ]
slow [sləʊ]	grow [grəʊ]		

Lesson 2　Homework

Ⅰ. 英语书法练习。

1. 按照英语国际音标四线三格书写格式抄写[aɪ] [eɪ] [ɔɪ] [ɪə] [eə] [ʊə] [aʊ] [əʊ]各5遍。
2. 抄写26个英文字母中 Oo－Tt 各5遍，注意书写笔顺和字母占格。

Ⅱ. 跟读模仿以下单词发音，按要求提交模仿作业。

year [jɪə(r)]	deer [dɪə(r)]	idea [aɪˈdɪə]	here [hɪə(r)]
sure [ʃʊə(r)]	poor [pʊə(r)]	tour [tʊə(r)]	unusual [ʌnˈjuːʒʊəl]
chair [tʃeə(r)]	bear [beə(r)]	care [keə(r)]	where [weə(r)]
main [meɪn]	pay [peɪ]	eight [eɪt]	great [greɪt]
fine [faɪn]	fly [flaɪ]	die [daɪ]	night [naɪt]
soil [sɔɪl]	toy [tɔɪ]	voice [vɔɪs]	noisy [ˈnɔɪzi]
mouse [maʊs]	cow [kaʊ]	shout [ʃaʊt]	cloud [klaʊd]
hero [ˈhɪərəʊ]	boat [bəʊt]	toe [təʊ]	yellow [ˈjeləʊ]

Ⅲ. 跟读模仿下列对话，按要求提交模仿作业。

Sarah: Hi, Nicole. What are you up to?

Nicole: Oh, just walking. Are you here for a walk, too?

Sarah: That's right. I'm a bit bored at home.

Nicole: Me too. We can walk together if you want.

Sarah: Cool! Oh no—look out! Mike Smith is coming. I don't like him!

Nicole: Come on. Let's walk over here.

Sarah: I don't want him to see me. Hurry up, Nicole!

Lesson 3　Consonants Ⅰ　辅音(一)

Ⅰ. [p] & [b] Plosive consonants 爆破音

1. [p]

1) Manner of articulation 发音要领

When the sound is made, the lips are slightly closed, the air stream is compressed in the oral cavity, the airflow is rapidly ejected from the mouth, and the vocal cords are not vibrating.

发此音时,双唇轻轻闭合,在口腔内压迫气流,然后将气流快速从口腔喷出,不振动声带。

2) Practice 发音练习

pen [pen]　　　　pear [peə(r)]　　　　　price [praɪs]　　please [pliːz]
parent [ˈpeərnt]　party [ˈpɑːti]　　　　　map [mæp]　　 help [help]
tape [teɪp]　　　 computer [kəmˈpjuːtə(r)]　purple [ˈpɜːpl]

2. [b]

1) Manner of articulation 发音要领

When this sound is made, it is very similar to that of [p]. The lips are slightly closed, press the airflow in the mouth, and then release the airflow rapidly from the mouth, vibrating the vocal cords.

发此音时,与发[p]非常相像,双唇轻轻闭合,在口腔内压迫气流,然后将气流快速从口腔喷出,但需振动声带。

2) Practice 发音练习

bad [bæd]　　　　　　bed [bed]　　　　　　bat [bæt]
blue [bluː]　　　　　　because [bɪˈkɒz]　　　busy [ˈbɪzi]
banana [bəˈnɑːnə]　　library [ˈlaɪbrəri]　　number [ˈnʌmbə(r)]
baseball [ˈbeɪsbɔːl]

Ⅱ. [t] & [d] Plosive consonants 爆破音

1. [t]

1) Manner of articulation 发音要领

When this sound is made, the lips are closed with the tip of the tongue against the upper gum to form air obstacles, and then let the air suddenly bomb out of the mouth, without vibration of the vocal cords.

发此音时，双唇未开，舌尖抵住上齿龈，形成气流阻碍，然后将气流快速从口腔弹出来，不振动声带。

2) Practice 发音练习

table [ˈteɪbl]　　　　take [teɪk]　　　tape [teɪp]　　　tell [tel]
telephone [ˈtelɪfəʊn]　tennis [ˈtenɪs]　tidy [ˈtaɪdi]　　sweater [ˈswetə(r)]
late [leɪt]　　　　　　carrot [ˈkærət]

2. [d]

1) Manner of articulation 发音要领

The pronunciation method is the same as that of [t], except that it is a voiced sound. When the sound is made, vibrate the vocal cords. It is very similar to the initial consonant "d" in Chinese.

发音要领和[t]一样，只不过它是一个浊音，需要振动声带，和汉语的声母"d"非常相似。

2) Practice 发音练习

dad [dæd]　　　　dead [ded]　　　　bad [bæd]　　　　good [gʊd]

guide [gaɪd]　　　die [daɪ]　　　　 down [daʊn]　　　dance [dɑːns]

today [təˈdeɪ]　　 under [ˈʌndə(r)]

Ⅲ. [k] & [g] Plosive consonants 爆破音

1. [k]

1) Manner of articulation 发音要领

When this sound is made, the lips slightly open. The tongue backs up to form an obstruction, and then let the air suddenly bomb out of the mouth to form a plosive sound without vibrating the vocal cords.

发此音时,双唇微开。舌后部抬起,形成阻碍,然后让气流突然冲出口腔,发出爆破音,不振动声带。

2) Practice 发音练习

can [kæn]　　　　cry [kraɪ]　　　　cool [kuːl]　　　cute [kjuːt]

kill [kɪl]　　　　 keep [kiːp]　　　 duck [dʌk]　　　sick [sɪk]

walk [wɔːk]　　　homework [ˈhəʊmwɜːk]　　knock [nɒk]

2. [g]

1) Manner of articulation 发音要领

When this sound is made, it is very similar to that of [k]. The lips are ajar, the tongue backs up to form an obstruction, and then let the air suddenly bomb out of the mouth to form a plosive sound, vibrating the vocal cords.

发此音时,与发[k]非常相像,双唇微开,舌后部抬起,形成阻碍,然后让气流突然冲出口腔,发出爆破音,但振动声带。

2) Practice 发音练习

go [gəʊ]　　　　　goal [gəʊl]　　　　gold [gəʊld]　　　good [gʊd]

get [get]　　　　great [greɪt]　　　game [geɪm]　　　egg [eg]
forget [fəˈget]　　dog [dɒg]　　　　leg [leg]　　　　flag [flæg]

Ⅳ. [f] & [v] Fricative consonants 摩擦音

1. [f]

1) Manner of articulation 发音要领

The lower lip touches the upper teeth slightly, and the air flows through the space between the lip and the teeth to form a friction sound. [f] is a voiceless consonant; the vocal cords do not vibrate.

发音时下唇轻触上齿,气流由唇齿间通过,形成摩擦音。[f]是清辅音,声带不振动。

2) Practice 发音练习

fire [ˈfaɪə(r)]　　finish [ˈfɪnɪʃ]　　find [faɪnd]　　friend [frend]
front [frʌnt]　　　left [left]　　　　office [ˈɒfɪs]　　half [hɑːf]
photo [ˈfəʊtəʊ]　　cough [kɒf]

2. [v]

1) Manner of articulation 发音要领

The lower lip touches the upper teeth slightly, and the air flows through the space between the lip and the teeth to form a friction sound. [v] is a voiced consonant; the vocal cords vibrate.

发音时下唇轻触上齿,气流由唇齿间通过,形成摩擦音。[v]是浊辅音,声带振动。

2) Practice 发音练习

very [ˈveri]　　violin [ˌvaɪəˈlɪn]　　visit [ˈvɪzɪt]　　five [faɪv]
move [muːv]　　save [seɪv]　　　　　lovely [ˈlʌvli]　　living [ˈlɪvɪŋ]

V. [s] & [z] Fricative consonants 摩擦音

1. [s]

1) Manner of articulation 发音要领

When the sound is made, a narrow gap is formed when the tip and the upper part of the tongue go near the upper gum, and the air flows out of the narrow seam and is rubbed into a sound. However, aspirate without vibrating the vocal cords.

发此音时,舌尖及舌中靠近上齿龈形成窄缝,气流从窄缝中流出,摩擦成音。但是,只送气,不振动声带。

2) Practice 发音练习

son [sʌn]　　　　sunny [ˈsʌni]　　　school [skuːl]　　　study [ˈstʌdi]

sport [spɔːt]　　student [ˈstjuːdnt]　soup [suːp]　　　　rice [raɪs]

place [pleɪs]　　miss [mɪs]

2. [z]

1) Manner of articulation 发音要领

When the sound is made, the shapes of the tongue and the mouth are the same as those of [s]. The difference is that the vocal cords need to vibrate, but don't aspirate.

发[z]音和发[s]音时的舌形和口形相同,不同的是发此音时声带需要振动,但不送气。

2) Practice 发音练习

zoo [zuː]　　　　　　zero [ˈzɪərəʊ]　　　easy [ˈiːzi]

lazy [ˈleɪzi]　　　　　size [saɪz]　　　　　does [dʌz]

sometimes [ˈsʌmtaɪmz]　please [pliːz]　　　exercise [ˈeksəsaɪz]

as [əz; æz]

VI. [θ] & [ð] Fricative consonants 摩擦音

1. [θ]

1) Manner of articulation 发音要领

When the sound is made, the lips slightly open, put out the tongue, the upper and the lower teeth slightly bite the tip of the tongue, and then blow the air out of the seams in the teeth without vibrating the vocal cords.

发此音时,双唇微开,舌头伸出,上下齿轻咬住舌尖,将气流从牙齿的缝隙中吹出来,声带不振动。

2) Practice 发音练习

three [θriː]   thin [θɪn]   thank [θæŋk]   north [nɔːθ]
south [saʊθ]   health [helθ]   tooth [tuːθ]   cloth [klɒθ]
month [mʌnθ]   birthday [ˈbɜːθdeɪ]

2. [ð]

1) Manner of articulation 发音要领

The lips slightly open, the teeth bite the tip of the tongue slightly, block the airflow, allow only a small amount of air to blow out from the seams in the teeth, and the vocal cords vibrate.

双唇微开,上下齿轻咬住舌尖,让气流尽量被上下齿堵住,只允许少量气体从牙齿缝隙中吹出来,同时振动声带发出声音。

2) Practice 发音练习

this [ðɪs]   that [ðæt]   these [ðiːz]
those [ðəʊz]   there [ðeə(r)]   then [ðen]
father [ˈfɑːðə(r)]   mother [ˈmʌðə(r)]   brother [ˈbrʌðə(r)]
weather [ˈweðə(r)]   with [wɪð]

Ⅶ. [ʃ] & [ʒ] Fricative consonants 摩擦音

1. [ʃ]

1) Manner of articulation 发音要领

When the sound is made, the lips protrude forward, the upper and lower teeth move close, the tip of the tongue rises upward to the posterior part of the gum, the tongue rises, and then blow outward without vibrating the vocal cords.

发此音时，双唇翘起向前突出，上下齿靠拢，舌尖抬向上齿龈较后部位，舌身抬高，然后向外吹气，不振动声带。

2) Practice 发音练习

shy [ʃaɪ]　　　　　sure [ʃʊə(r)]　　　　shout [ʃaʊt]　　　　Russian [ˈrʌʃn]
social [ˈsəʊʃl]　　　delicious [dɪˈlɪʃəs]　station [ˈsteɪʃn]　　wish [wɪʃ]

2. [ʒ]

1) Manner of articulation 发音要领

When the sound is made, the shape of the mouth is the same as that of [ʃ]. The difference is that the sound is unaspirated, but the vocal cords vibrate. (The lips protrude forward, the upper and lower teeth move close, the tip of the tongue rises upward to the posterior part of the gum, and the tongue rises.)

发[ʒ]时与发[ʃ]时的口形相同，不同之处在于此音不送气，振动声带。(双唇翘起向前突出，上下齿靠拢，舌尖抬向上齿龈较后部位，舌身抬高。)

2) Practice 发音练习

usual [ˈjuːʒʊəl]　　　usually [ˈjuːʒʊəli]　　　decision [dɪˈsɪʒn]
vision [ˈvɪʒn]　　　　television [ˈtelɪvɪʒn]　　measure [ˈmeʒə(r)]
leisure [leʒə(r)]　　　treasure [ˈtreʒə(r)]　　　pleasure [ˈpleʒə(r)]
massage [ˈmæsɑːʒ]

Lesson 3　Homework

Ⅰ. 英语书法练习。

1. 按照英语国际音标四线三格书写格式抄写[p] [b] [t] [d] [k] [g] [f] [v] [s] [z] [θ] [ð] [ʃ] [ʒ]各5遍。
2. 抄写26个英文字母中 Uu−Zz 各5遍，注意书写笔顺和字母占格。

Ⅱ. 跟读模仿以下单词发音，按要求提交模仿作业。

price [praɪs]	pig [pɪg]	apple [ˈæpl]
app [æp]	beach [biːtʃ]	bear [beə(r)]
rubber [ˈrʌbə(r)]	bubble [ˈbʌbl]	torch [tɔːtʃ]
right [raɪt]	letter [ˈletə(r)]	bottle [ˈbɒtl]
die [daɪ]	duck [dʌk]	add [æd]
address [əˈdres]	kiss [kɪs]	call [kɔːl]
occur [əˈkɜː]	luck [lʌk]	tiger [ˈtaɪgə(r)]
egg [eg]	guess [ges]	ghost [gəʊst]
football [ˈfʊtbɔːl]	office [ˈɒfɪs]	photo [ˈfəʊtəʊ]
half [hɑːf]	voice [vɔɪs]	love [lʌv]
think [θɪŋk]	tooth [tuːθ]	clothes [kləʊðz]
mother [ˈmʌðə(r)]	sure [ʃʊə(r)]	ship [ʃɪp]
chef [ʃef]	special [ˈspeʃl]	social [ˈsəʊʃl]
patient [ˈpeɪʃnt]	measure [ˈmeʒə(r)]	massage [ˈmæsɑːʒ]
decision [dɪˈsɪʒn]	some [sʌm]	class [klɑːs]
scene [siːn]	city [ˈsɪti]	zero [ˈzɪərəʊ]
jazz [dʒæz]	desert [ˈdezət]	rose [rəʊz]

Ⅲ. 跟读模仿下列对话,按要求提交模仿作业。

A: Hello. Can I help you?
B: Yes, please. I like these shoes. Have you got them in black?
A: Yes, we have.
B: Great. Can I try them on?
A: Yes, of course. What size do you take?
B: I'm a size 42... They're very nice. I'll take them. How much are they?
A: They're £75.
B: I don't have cash. Can I pay with my contactless card?
A: Yes, of course.

Lesson 4　Consonants Ⅱ 辅音(二)

Ⅰ. [ts] & [dz] Affricate consonants 破擦音

1. [ts]

1) Manner of articulation 发音要领

When the sound is made, the tip of the tongue is put against the upper gum, first do not sound; the tongue immediately leaves the upper gum, and moves to the down gum. The air flows out of the gap between the tongue and the upper and lower gums; the vocal cords do not vibrate, make the sound and aspirate.

发此音时,舌尖抵住上齿龈,先不发声;舌尖立即离开上齿龈,移向下齿龈。气流从舌头和上下齿龈间的缝隙流出;声带不振动,发音送气。

2) Practice 发音练习

cats [kæts]	hats [hæts]	meets [mi:ts]	eats [i:ts]
tents [tents]	gets [gets]	lots [lɒts]	starts [stɑ:ts]
gifts [gɪfts]	kites [kaɪts]		

2. [dz]

1) Manner of articulation 发音要领

When the sound is made, the shapes of the tongue and the mouth are the same as those of [ts], but the vocal cords need to vibrate, and do not aspirate. The sound explodes out with rapid and powerful force.

发音时的舌形和口形与[ts]一样,但是需要振动声带,且不送气。发音时

Lesson 4　Consonants Ⅱ　辅音(二)

是急促有力,爆破而出。

2) Practice 发音练习

beds [bedz]　　　heads [hedz]　　　　feeds [fiːdz]　　　reads [riːdz]
friends [frendz]　weekends [ˌwiːk'endz]　cards [kɑːdz]　　birds [bɜːdz]
hands [hændz]　　roads [rəʊdz]

Ⅱ. [tʃ] & [dʒ] Affricate consonants 破擦音

1. [tʃ]

1) Manner of articulation 语音要领

When the sound is made, the tip and the blade of the tongue are put against the upper gum and tooth edge to form obstacles. At the same time, lift the front part of the tongue, getting ready to sound fricative. Once the occlusion is released, the air flows out of the narrow seam, and the lips slightly square. The vocal cords do not vibrate, but aspirate.

发此音时,先将舌尖、舌叶及舌边抵住上齿龈及边齿,形成阻塞。同时,舌前部抬高,做好发摩擦音的准备。一旦闭塞部位松开,气流即从舌面上方的窄缝中摩擦而出,双唇略呈方形。声带不振动,需送气。

2) Practice 发音练习

chicken ['tʃɪkɪn]　　　　child [tʃaɪld]　　　　chess [tʃes]
kitchen ['kɪtʃɪn]　　　　teacher ['tiːtʃə(r)]　　nature ['neɪtʃə(r)]
picture ['pɪktʃə(r)]　　　Dutch ['dʌtʃ]　　　　watch [wɒtʃ]
March [mɑːtʃ]　　　　　question ['kwestʃən]

2. [dʒ]

1) Manner of articulation 发音要领

When the sound is made, the shapes of the tongue and the tongue and the mouth are the same as those of [tʃ], but the vocal cords need to vibrate.

发音时的舌形、口形和[tʃ]一致,但不同的是发音时需要振动声带。

2) Practice 发音练习

jump [dʒʌmp]　　　　just [dʒʌst]　　　　　juice [dʒuːs]

job [dʒɒb]　　　　　 judge [dʒʌdʒ]　　　　 bridge[brɪdʒ]

giraffe [dʒəˈrɑːf]　　 geography [dʒɪˈɒgrəfi]　 danger[ˈdeɪndʒə(r)]

vegetable [ˈvedʒtəbl]　orange [ˈɒrɪndʒ]　　　 village[ˈvɪlɪdʒ]

Ⅲ. [tr] & [dr] Affricate consonants 破擦音

1. [tr]

1) Manner of articulation 发音要领

When the sound is made, the back of the tongue is sunken, and the front of the tongue is folded and turned upward. It is obstructed by contacting with the back part of the upper gum and the side teeth, and the tongue becomes concave. The air bursts, a slit is formed and the friction sound is made, with lips slightly pursed like playing the flute. The vocal cords do not vibrate, but aspirate.

发此音时,舌头后部下陷,舌头前部收拢上翘,与上齿龈后部和边齿接触形成阻塞,整个舌头成为凹形。待气流冲开,形成狭缝而摩擦成音,双唇稍稍噘起如吹笛状,发[tr]时,声带不振动,要送气。

2) Practice 发音练习

tree [triː]　　　　trip [trɪp]　　　　true[truː]　　　　trousers [ˈtraʊzəz]

train [treɪn]　　　street [striːt]　　 strict [strɪkt]　　 Australia[ɒˈstreɪlɪə]

2. [dr]

1) Manner of articulation 发音要领

When the sound is made, the shapes of the tongue and the mouth are the same as those of [tr], but the vocal cords need to vibrate, and do not aspirate.

发此音时,舌形、口形与发[tr]时一样,但不同的是发[dr]时声带振动,不送气。

2) Practice 发音练习

draw [drɔː]   drop [drɒp]   dry [draɪ]   dragon ['drægən]
drama ['drɑːmə]   drum [drʌm]   drink [drɪŋk]   drunk [drʌŋk]
dress [dres]   dream [driːm]

Ⅳ. [h] Fricative consonant 摩擦音

1) Manner of articulation 发音要领

When the sound is made, the mouth is half opened, the upper and lower teeth are also opened, and the tongue rests naturally flat, without vibration of the vocal cords. At the same time, breathe outward.

发此音时,嘴半开,上下齿亦开,舌头自然平放,不振动声带,同时向外呵气,摩擦成音。

2) Practice 发音练习

he [hiː]   his [hɪz]   history ['hɪstri]   hat [hæt]
have [hæv]   hot [hɒt]   height [haɪt]   hard [hɑːd]
healthy ['helθi]   who [huː]

Ⅴ. [l] Lateral consonant 舌侧音

1) Manner of articulation 发音要领

When the sound is made, the mouth is slightly open, the tip of the tongue is put against the upper gum, but the posterior part of the tongue tip is slightly raised, vibrate vocal cords, and air flow vents from both sides of the tongue.

• There are two cases:

a. [l] in front of the vowel: it is called clear tongue lateral, like "like".
b. [l] behind the vowel: it is called fuzzy tongue lateral, but the tip of the

tongue must be raised, put against the upper gum, like "hall".

发音时,口腔微微张开,舌尖抵上齿龈,但舌尖后部稍稍抬起,振动声带,气流从舌头的两侧泄出。

- 发音时要分为两种情况:

a. [l]在元音前:叫作清晰舌边音,如在"like"中的发音。

b. [l]在元音后:叫作模糊舌边音,需要注意的是,舌尖一定要翘起,抵住上齿龈,如在"hall"中的发音。

2) Practice 发音练习

long [lɒŋ]	listen [ˈlɪsən]	police [pəˈliːs]	world [wɜːld]
while [waɪl]	blow [bləʊ]	follow [ˈfɒləʊ]	allow [əˈlaʊ]
hall [hɔːl]	small [smɔːl]	girl [gɜːl]	

VI. [r] Fricative consonant 摩擦音

1) Manner of articulation 发音要领

When the sound is made, the lips open and slightly purse, the tip of the tongue rises, lifting up to the upper gum at the rear, the front part of the tongue (the tongue tip and both sides of the tongue) forms a concave, the air leaks above the tongue, and vibrate the vocal cords.

发此音时,双唇张开并微微噘起,舌尖上扬,向上齿龈后部抬起,舌前部(舌尖和舌身两侧)形成凹形,气流从舌面上方泄出,同时振动声带发声。

2) Practice 发音练习

| rich [rɪtʃ] | road [rəʊd] | right [raɪt] | red [red] |
| race [reɪs] | eraser [ɪˈreɪzə(r)] | free [friː] | across [əˈkrɒs] |

VII. [m] Nasal consonant 鼻音

1) Manner of articulation 发音要领

When the sound is made, the lips are closed, the tongue is flat, the vocal cords are vibrating, and the air is released from the nasal passage. Do not open your mouth.

发[m]时,双唇紧闭,舌头放平,振动声带,让气流从鼻腔通道泄出。注意不张嘴。

2) Practice 发音练习

many [ˈmeni]   much [mʌtʃ]   must [mʌst]
mother [ˈmʌðə(r)] mouth [maʊθ]   may [meɪ]
classmate [ˈklɑːsmeɪt] smart [smɑːt] number [ˈnʌmbə(r)]
cream [kriːm]

VIII. [n] Nasal consonant 鼻音

1) Manner of articulation 发音要领

When the sound is made, the lips are slightly open, the tip of the tongue rises, gently touching the upper gum, vibrate the vocal cords, and the airflow is coming out of the nasal cavity.

发[n]时,双唇微张,舌尖上扬,轻轻抵住上齿龈,振动声带,气流由鼻腔出来。

2) Practice 发音练习

north [nɔːθ]   nice [naɪs]   nine [naɪn]   no [nəʊ]
know [nəʊ]   kind [kaɪnd]   lunch [lʌntʃ]   uniform [ˈjuːnɪfɔːm]
learn [lɜːn]   turn [tɜːn]

IX. [ŋ] Nasal consonant 鼻音

1) Manner of articulation 发音要领

When the sound is made, the tongue root is raised to block the air, so the air flows into the nasal cavity, exhales from the nose, and vibrate the vocal cords at the same time.

发[ŋ]时,舌根抬高以形成阻碍堵住气流,使得气流流入鼻腔,从鼻呼出,同时振动声带。

2. Practice 发音练习

doing [ˈduːɪŋ]　　　anything [ˈenɪθɪŋ]　　　sing [sɪŋ]　　　song [sɒŋ]
young [jʌŋ]　　　bank [bæŋk]　　　drink [drɪŋk]　　　think [θɪŋk]
thanks [θæŋks]　　　language [ˈlæŋgwɪdʒ]

Ⅹ. [w] Semi-vowel 半元音

1) Manner of articulation 发音要领

When the sound is made, the back of the tongue is raised, and the lips are rounded to allow the airflow to exhale freely from the mouth, and vibrate the vocal cords.

发[w]时,舌后部抬高,双唇收圆突出,让气流从口腔自由呼出,声带振动。

2) Practice 发音练习

winter [ˈwɪntə(r)]　　　wind [wɪnd]　　　windy [ˈwɪndi]　　　work [wɜːk]
weather [ˈweðə(r)]　　　why [waɪ]　　　what [wɒt]　　　when [wen]
while [waɪl]　　　swim [swɪm]

Ⅺ. [j] Semi-vowel 半元音

1) Manner of articulation 发音要领

When the sound is made, the middle of the tongue is raised, the lip shape and tongue position are close to those of [ɪ]. The airflow is exhaled freely from the mouth and the vocal cords vibrate.

发[j]音时,舌中部抬高,使唇形和舌位接近于[ɪ],气流从口腔自由呼出,声带振动。

2) Practice 发音练习

year [jɪə(r)]　　　yeah [jeə]　　　yes [jes]　　　yesterday [ˈjestədeɪ] yellow [ˈjeləʊ]　　yard [jɑːd]　　use [juːz]　　usually [ˈjuːʒʊəli]

Lesson 4　Homework

Ⅰ. 英语书法练习。

按照英语国际音标四线三格书写格式抄写[ts] [dz] [tʃ] [dʒ] [tr] [dr] [m] [n] [ŋ] [w] [j] [r] [h] [l]各5遍。

Ⅱ. 跟读模仿以下单词发音，按要求提交模仿作业。

check [tʃek]	catch [kætʃ]	chess [tʃes]	China [ˈtʃaɪnə]
jump [dʒʌmp]	gem [dʒem]	orange [ˈɒrɪndʒ]	bridge [brɪdʒ]
pants [pænts]	cats [kæts]	rats [ræts]	mats [mæts]
cards [kɑːdz]	friends [frendz]	birds [bɜːdz]	beds [bedz]
tree [triː]	trouble [ˈtrʌbl]	trip [trɪp]	trace [treɪs]
drivers [ˈdraɪvə(r)z]	drum [drʌm]	drag [dræg]	driver [ˈdraɪvə(r)]
mouse [maʊs]	farm [fɑːm]	map [mæp]	moon [muːn]
thin [θɪn]	train [treɪn]	knock [nɒk]	knee [niː]
pink [pɪŋk]	wink [wɪŋk]	king [kɪŋ]	sing [sɪŋ]
why [waɪ]	woke [wəʊk]	witch [wɪtʃ]	why [waɪ]
yearn [jɜːn]	year [jɪə(r)]	yet [jet]	yellow [ˈjeləʊ]
read [riːd]	green [griːn]	rich [rɪtʃ]	catch [kætʃ]
hand [hænd]	hope [həʊp]	his [hɪz]	heart [hɑːt]
light [laɪt]	lake [leɪk]	ball [bɔːl]	full [fʊl]

Ⅲ. 跟读模仿下列对话，按要求提交模仿作业。

Dad: Hi, Jordan! I'm home.

Jordan: Hi, Dad!

Dad: So, what are you doing?

Jordan: I'm making pizza — for me and my friends.

Dad: Hmmm ... What about me?

Jordan: I'm really sorry, Dad. It's just for us.

Dad: Oh right. Look at this kitchen! What a mess!

Jordan: Sorry, Dad. But don't worry! I'm finishing now!

Dad: OK then. Now, how can I help?

Jordan: Actually, I'm OK. It's just a pizza.

Dad: Onion? Red pepper? Just that? We can make that better, I'm sure.

Jordan: Really?

Dad: Let's add a couple of mushrooms. There we are.

Jordan: But I don't like mushrooms.

Dad: So what? You can always take them off. I think you need some chilli pepper as well.

Jordan: Dad, stop it. It's horrible. Thanks a lot.

Dad: Are you upset with me? Now I feel bad. I just wanted to help.

Jordan: Don't worry, Dad. We can just eat crisps.

Dad: No, you can't. You can eat pizza. Get me the phone and I'll order one. Ice cream, too!

Jordan: Really, Dad? Thanks!

Dad: And I can eat this one here!

Lesson 5　Mixed practice of vowels and consonants 元音辅音混合练习

Ⅰ. Mixed practice of phonemes 音标混合练习

Group 1：　[ɔː]　[iː]　[æ]　[ɑː]　[ɔː]　[p]　[t]　[k]

Group 2：　[ə]　[e]　[uː]　[θ]　[ʃ]　[dʒ]　[ŋ]　[dr]

Group 3：　[ɜː]　[eɪ]　[ɒɪ]　[eə]　[h]　[n]　[l]　[ʊ]

Group 4：　[ɪ]　[ə]　[ʊ]　[aɪ]　[b]　[d]　[g]　[v]

Group 5：　[ʊ]　[əʊ]　[ɪə]　[ð]　[s]　[tʃ]　[r]　[f]

Group 6：　[ʌ]　[ɒ]　[aʊ]　[ʊə]　[z]　[ʒ]　[j]　[w]

Group 7：　[æ]　[ɔː]　[eɪ]　[tʃ]　[m]　[r]　[tr]　[ʃ]

Ⅱ. The pronunciation of letters and combination of letters 字母和字母组合的发音

元音字母以及元音字母组合的发音

The pronunciation of vowels and combination of vowels

元音字母	位置	读音	例　　词	例外
a	重读开音节	[eɪ]	Dale same name make tape plane late take sale save race	
	重读闭音节	[æ]	am map bag dad hat bat fat pancake	

续表

元音字母	位置	读音	例词	例外
a	非重读音节	[ə]	China Gina afraid arrival across along vegetable Canada cinema	have [æ] vase [ɑː] water [ɔː]
		[ɪ]	village cabbage courage	
	在[w]后	[ɒ]	want wash watch what	
	在 st, sk, ss, th, nch, f, nc 前	[ɑː]	last past fast ask task class glasses father path branch after giraffe dance	
	特殊情况	[e]	any many anything anybody	
e	重读开音节	[iː]	be he me we these she Chinese	
	重读闭音节	[e]	bed get let red ten hotel pet	
	非重读音节	[ə]	hello actress excellent problem open children	
		[ɪ]	because eraser behind between excuse describe expensive relax	
i(y)	重读开音节	[aɪ]	five nice nine price rice time arrive crime drive fire kite life like ride size	give [ɪ] live [ɪ] pyramid [ɪ]
	重读闭音节	[ɪ]	big fifth his sister sit winter picture	
	y 在重读音节中	[aɪ]	by dry fly cycle sky shy why	
	y 在非重读音节中	[i]	busy family happy only party twenty any baby candy curly city healthy	
	在 nd, ld, mb 前	[aɪ]	find mind kind blind child climb	
	非重读音节	[ə]	family terrible possible horrible	
	在下列单词中	[iː]	police magazine machine technique	
o	重读开音节	[əʊ]	no so go home ago stone note progress motor lonely smoke joke	woman [ʊ] women [ɪ]
	重读闭音节	[ɒ]	not hot lot stop shop job dog lost	
	在 n, m, v, th 前	[ʌ]	son onion front come some love cover brother mother another	
	在以 ld, st, th 结尾的一些词中	[əʊ]	hold fold told host most almost both	

续表

元音字母	位置	读音	例词	例外
o	非重读音节	[ə]	tonight tomato official position	
	在下列单词中	[uː]	move who do to movie prove lose whose shoe remove	
u	重读开音节	[juː]	cute use duty computer reduce Tuesday	true [uː] busy [ɪ] bury [e] minute [ɪ]
	重读闭音节	[ʌ]	but cup us up number run bus club cut sun	
		[ʊ]	put pull push full bullet	
	非重读音节	[ə]	until unless	
	在开音节中,在辅音字母 l,r,j 后	[uː]	blue rude rule ruler June	

元音字母组合	位置	读音	例词	例外
ar	重读	[ɑː]	car card far farm March party artist park guitar hard	
	在 w 后	[ɔː]	warm warn reward war	
	非重读	[ə]	dollar grammar	
er	重读	[ɜː]	her term person certain serve	
	非重读	[ə]	burger dinner number answer center danger later under	
or	重读	[ɔː]	for morning short forty horse form important corner	
	在 w 后	[ɜː]	work word world worth	
	非重读	[ə]	mirror doctor forbid forget	
ur	重读	[ɜː]	purple curly church Thursday nurse turn return	
	非重读	[ə]	surprise surround murmur	
ir	重读	[ɜː]	thirsty dirty first girl	

续表

元音字母组合		位置	读音	例词	例外
a	ai	重读音节	[eɪ]	rain straight wait remain sail praise raise brain	said [e]
		非重读音节	[ɪ]	captain	
			[ə]	mauntain	
	au		[ɔ:]	cause	aunt [ɑ:]
	al		[ɔ:]	also always walk ball talk	half [ɑ:]
	aw		[ɔ:]	draw saw dawn	
	air		[eə]	fair hair upstairs	
	are		[eə]	dare share compare careful	are [ɑ:]
	augh		[ɔ:]	taught caught daughter naughty	laugh [ɑ:f]
	ay	重读音节	[eɪ]	stay play say way today	says [e]
		非重读音节	[ɪ]	Sunday Monday	
e	ea		[i:]	please easy dream disease eat cream leave meat teach	
			[e]	breakfast sweater weather headache heavy healthy	
		特殊	[eɪ]	great break	
			[ɪə]	real idea theatre	
	ee		[i:]	green see meet week beef feed feel street	
	ear		[ɪə]	clear near hear dear ear year	
			[ɜ:]	heard learn earn early search	heart [ɑ:]
			[eə]	pear wear bear	
	ei		[i:]	receive ceiling seize	
	ew		[ju:]	few new news	sew [əʊ]
		在[l][r]后	[u:]	blew flew threw drew	
	ere		[eə]	there where	here [ɪə]

Lesson 5 Mixed practice of vowels and consonants 元音辅音混合练习

续表

元音字母组合		位置	读音	例词	例外
e	ey	重读音节	[eɪ]	grey hey obey	key [iː]
		非重读音节	[ɪ]	monkey donkey	
	eigh		[eɪ]	weight eight eighty	height [aɪ]
i	ie		[iː]	piece thief field chief	diet [aɪə]
			[aɪ]	lie tie die	quiet [aɪə]
	ire		[aɪə]	hire tire wire	
	igh		[aɪ]	right fight night high bright light	
o	oa		[əʊ]	road soap coat boat	broad [ɔː] abroad [ɔː]
	oi		[ɔɪ]	voice noise point choice	
	oy		[ɔɪ]	toy boy enjoy	
	oo	在 k, d 前	[ʊ]	took look cook stood wood good	food [uː] flood [ʌ] blood [ʌ]
		在其他字母前	[uː]	roof cool soon choose school	wool [ʊ] foot [ʊ]
	oor		[ɔː]	floor door	poor [ʊə]
	ou		[aʊ]	pound house mountain trousers south thousand	shoulder [əʊ] soul [əʊ]
			[ʌ]	cousin couple double country touch trouble	
			[uː]	route group soup	
			[ʊ]	could should would	
	ough		[ɔː]	fought bought brought thought	though [əʊ] plough [aʊ] cough [ɒf] through [uː] thorough [ə] enough [ʌf]

续表

元音字母组合		位置	读音	例词	例外
o	ow		[aʊ]	now cow brown town down flower	knowledge [ɒ]
			[əʊ]	blow follow snow window row owner low show throw grow	
u	ure	重读音节	[ʊə]	sure surely	
		非重读音节	[ə]	pleasure nature	

辅音字母以及辅音字母组合的发音
The pronunciation of consonants and combination of consonants

辅音字母	位置	读音	例　词	例外
b	在 m 后或在 t 之前	不发音	comb climb doubt	
	其他情况	[b]	bed bag big busy boring	
c	在 e, i, y 前	[s]	centre office rice percent concert city decide bicycle	
	在 ia, ie 前	[ʃ]	social especial ancient	
	其他情况	[k]	color class cause capital	
g	在以 n 结尾的词中	不发音	sign foreign	garage [ʒ] get [g]
	在 e, i, y 前	[dʒ]	geography large general page giant gym	
	其他情况	[g]	game great gift girl goal glad	
h	一般情况	[h]	habit history hall hundred	
	在个别词中	不发音	honest hour honor	
k	一般情况	[k]	keep kill kind kite walk key	
	在 n 前	不发音	know knife	

Lesson 5　Mixed practice of vowels and consonants 元音辅音混合练习

续表

辅音字母	位置	读音	例　词	例外
s	词首	[s]	salad sale soccer sound subject	
	在元音字母和元音字母之间	[z]	please those visit music	base [s] useful [s]
	在词中清辅音前	[s]	ask test sister lost last	
	在词中浊辅音前	[z]	Tuesday husband	
	在元音字母 u, i 前	[ʃ]	sure sugar Russia Asia	
	在 u, ion 前	[ʒ]	pleasure usually television occasion	
n	在字母 k, x, g 前	[ŋ]	think thank bank anxious finger	strange[n]
	在其他字母前	[n]	banana need corner nine nice line	
x	在元音字母前	[gz]	exam example exist exactly	
	在其他字母前	[ks]	excuse sixty except text	

辅音字母组合	位置	读音	例　词	例外
ch		[tʃ]	chair chicken cheap chess march choose chalk change	sandwich [dʒ]
		[k]	Christmas headache school	
		[ʃ]	machine moustache	
tch		[tʃ]	watch kitchen match	
th		[θ]	think thank thing worth thirty Thursday mouth	
		[ð]	then with although those this that other weather	
qu		[kw]	quilt question quick quite	
ph		[f]	phone photo physics	
ck		[k]	luck pick quickly back	
kn		[n]	knife know knowledge knock	
ng		[ŋ]	crossing something sing	
wr		[r]	write wrong wrap wretch	
wh		[w]	when where white why	
	在字母 o 前	[h]	whole whose who whom	
tion	在词尾	[ʃən]	education vacation station	
	在字母 s 后	[tʃən]	suggestion question	
sion		[ʒən]	decision conclusion	

Lesson 5　Homework

Ⅰ. 跟读模仿以下单词发音，按要求提交模仿作业。

guitar [gɪˈtɑː]　　　　　lucky [ˈlʌki]　　　　　just [dʒʌst]
summer [ˈsʌmə(r)]　　　worry [ˈwʌri]　　　　jump [dʒʌmp]
uniform [ˈjuːnɪfɔːm]　　 across [əˈkrɒs]　　　 follow [ˈfɒləʊ]
forest [ˈfɒrɪst]　　　　　hospital [ˈhɒspɪtl]　　 afraid [əˈfreɪd]
America [əˈmerɪkə]　　 around [əˈraʊnd]　　 panda [ˈpændə]
different [ˈdɪfrənt]　　　either [ˈaɪðə(r)]　　　 flower [ˈflaʊə(r)]
remember [rɪˈmembə(r)] surprise [səˈpraɪz]　 tonight [təˈnaɪt]
violin [ˌvaɪəˈlɪn]　　　　 dirty [ˈdɜːti]　　　　　Africa [ˈæfrɪkə]
animal [ˈænɪml]　　　　important [ɪmˈpɔːtnt]　kitchen [ˈkɪtʃɪn]
porridge [ˈpɒrɪdʒ]

Ⅱ. 跟读模仿下列对话，按要求提交模仿作业。

John: I'm tired. Let's stop now, Mandy. I'm not so sure why we're doing this, to be honest.

Mandy: You know why, John. We're going to houses to sell these biscuits and the money goes to help homeless people.

John: I know.

Mandy: Hang on! This is Mrs Grundy's house. Let's not waste our time here. I don't think she'll give us any money. She's really unfriendly.

John: I know what you mean. Last week, she shouted at me and Ben because we were 'being noisy' in the street!

Mandy: Maybe she's just a bit lonely.

John: I know, but it's not really our problem. Come on.

Mrs Grundy: Hello! Can I help you?

Mandy: Um, hello. Well, we're selling biscuits to help homeless people.

Mrs Grundy: What a good idea. Can I buy some?

Mandy: Erm ... sure. They're two pounds for a bag.

Mrs Grundy: OK. Give me two bags. And here's ten pounds. Don't worry about any change, though. Bye!

Mandy: Wow. So, Mrs Grundy isn't so unfriendly after all. I was completely wrong!

John: Yes, we were wrong. But it's not a big deal. Anyway, that's ten pounds. We could stop now!

Mandy: I don't think that's a good idea, John. We've still got six bags to sell. Why don't we do another six houses? Then, how about playing tennis?

John: Great idea!

Lesson 6　Practice of monosyllables
单音节拼读练习

Ⅰ. Syllables 音节

The syllables are phonetic units composed of vowel phonemes. It is the basic unit of pronunciation, and the pronunciation of any word is broken down into syllables. In English, the vowel sound is so loud that a single vowel can form a syllable, and a vowel and a few consonants can also form a syllable.

Here are some common types of syllables:

- Vowel, e. g.　a [eɪ], I [aɪ] and so on.
- Consonant+vowel, e. g.　me [mi:], do [du:] and so on.
- Vowel+consonant, e. g.　in [ɪn], at [æt] and so on.
- Consonant+vowel+consonant, e. g.　hit [hɪt], speak [spi:k] and so on.

In addition, there is a special syllable in the English language that does not involve vowels but also constitutes syllables. Consonants [n] [l] are syllable consonants, with another consonant, such as [bl] [dl] [tl] [tn] [sl], can form a syllable, such as table ['teɪbl], middle ['mɪdl], bottle ['bɒtl], rotton ['rɒtn], pencil ['pensl], etc. This is the fifth way of making syllables:

Consonant+consonant [n] [l], for example, people ['pi:pl], little ['lɪtl].

音节是以元音音素为主体构成的发音单位。它是读音的基本单位,任何单词的读音,都是分解为一个个音节朗读。在英语中,元音特别响亮,一个元音可以构成一个音节,一个元音和一个或者几个辅音结合也可以构成一个音节。

常见的形式有:

- 元音,如 a [eɪ], I [aɪ]等。

- 辅音+元音,如 me [mi:], do [du:]等。
- 元音+辅音,如 in [ɪn], at [æt]等。
- 辅音+元音+辅音,如 hit [hɪt], speak [spi:k]等。

此外在英语里还有一种特殊音节,其构成没有元音的参与,但也构成音节。辅音[n][l]是成音节辅音,前面加上另一个辅音,如[bl] [dl] [tl] [tn] [sl],即可构成一个音节,如 table ['teɪbl], middle ['mɪdl], bottle ['bɒtl], rotton ['rɒtn], pencil ['pensl]等。此为音节构成的第五种方式,即:

辅音+辅音[n] [l],如 people ['pi:pl], little ['lɪtl]。

1. Open syllables 开音节

The open syllables are divided into absolute and relative open syllables.

1) Absolute open syllable: The syllable that ends with a vowel sound is called an absolute open syllable, e. g. hi [haɪ], me [mi:], go [gəʊ], flu [flu:], potato [pəteɪtəʊ].

2) Relative open syllable: The syllable that is formed by a vowel sound plus a consonant(except "r") and a silent vowel "e", e. g. nice [naɪs], name [neɪm], hole [həʊl], these [ði:z], muse [mju:z].

开音节分为绝对开音节和相对开音节。

1) 绝对开音节:以发音的元音字母结尾的音节叫作绝对开音节,如 hi [haɪ], me [mi:], go [gəʊ], flu [flu:], potato [pəteɪtəʊ]。

2) 相对开音节:一个元音字母加上一个辅音字母("r"除外),再加上不发音的元音字母"e"所构成的音节叫相对开音节,如 nice [naɪs], name [neɪm], hole [həʊl], these [ði:z], muse [mju:z]。

2. Closed syllables 闭音节

A closed syllable has one and only one vowel, and it ends in a consonant (except "r"). Examples include at [æt], bad [bæd], bet [bet], is [ɪz], hit [hɪt], soft [sɒft], us [ʌs], but [bʌt].

以辅音字母(r 除外)结尾的音节叫作闭音节,如 at [æt], bad [bæd], bet

[bet], is [ɪz], hit [hɪt], soft [sɒft], us [ʌs], but [bʌt]。

Ⅱ. Practice of one-syllable words 单音节单词练习

1	tea [tiː]	cup [kʌp]	pen [pen]	go [gəʊ]	they [ðeɪ]
2	am [æm]	at [æt]	eight [eɪt]	spell [spel]	each [iːtʃ]
3	ball [bɔːl]	late [leɪt]	big [bɪg]	use [juːz]	stop [stɒp]
4	nice [naɪs]	fight [faɪt]	break [breɪk]	draw [drɔː]	tooth [tuːθ]
5	guess [ges]	smart [smɑːt]	side [saɪd]	thin [θɪn]	same [seɪm]
6	dear [dɪə(r)]	class [klɑːs]	bear [beə(r)]	down [daʊn]	tree [triː]
7	chair [tʃeə(r)]	out [aʊt]	sure [ʃʊə(r)]	bat [bæt]	age [eɪdʒ]
8	tape [teɪp]	next [nekst]	can [kæn]	but [bʌt]	mouth [maʊθ]
9	drive [draɪv]	feet [fiːt]	cheer [tʃɪə(r)]	hair [heə(r)]	flag [flæg]
10	knife [naɪf]	bee [biː]	drop [drɒp]	need [niːd]	dance [dɑːns]
11	hear [hɪə(r)]	dress [dres]	height [haɪt]	kid [kɪd]	kite [kaɪt]
12	health [helθ]	light [laɪt]	laugh [lɑːf]	plane [pleɪn]	sport [spɔːt]
13	down [daʊn]	egg [eg]	job [dʒɒb]	price [praɪs]	more [mɔː]

续表

14	son [sʌn]	know [nəʊ]	house [haʊs]	meat [miːt]	end [end]
15	plate [pleɪt]	post [pəʊst]	park [paːk]	put [pʊt]	pool [puːl]
16	race [reɪs]	feel [fiːl]	reach [riːtʃ]	rope [rəʊp]	rule [ruːl]
17	save [seɪv]	swim [swɪm]	shy [ʃaɪ]	salt [sɒlt]	soon [suːn]
18	there [ðeə(r)]	this [ðɪs]	these [ðiːz]	thing [θɪŋ]	thank [θæŋk]
19	thin [θɪn]	three [θriː]	wake [weɪk]	why [waɪ]	wood [wʊd]
20	tie [taɪ]	such [sʌtʃ]	straight [streɪt]	sock [sɒk]	sharp [ʃaːp]

Lesson 6　Homework

Ⅰ. 跟读模仿以下单词发音,按要求提交模仿作业。

dance [daːns]　　past [paːst]　　smart [smaːt]　　hard [haːd]
large [laːdʒ]　　drum [drʌm]　　brush [brʌʃ]　　tall [tɔːl]
hall [hɔːl]　　person [ˈpɜːsn]　　dream [driːm]　　grow [grəʊ]
speak [spiːk]　　teach [tiːtʃ]　　street [striːt]　　tooth [tuːθ]
group [gruːp]　　wake [weɪk]　　town [taʊn]　　host [həʊst]
bus [bʌs]　　luck [lʌk]　　draw [drɔː]　　horse [hɔːs]

Ⅱ. 跟读模仿下列对话,按要求提交模仿作业。

Steve: So you've eaten here before?

Hannah: Yes, it's simple, but the food's great. It's perfect for a quick lunch.

Steve: What do they do?

Hannah: The rolls are great. You can choose two fillings from tomato, tuna, cheese, curried chicken and sweet corn. Or you can have more fillings if you want to pay extra.

Steve: And if I don't want a roll?

Hannah: The soups are good. Chicken and mushroom, potato and onion and a spicy red pepper one—it's really hot but it's delicious.

Steve: That sounds good.

Hannah: And we can't leave without having a cake. They've got some great cakes. Carrot, chocolate or a coffee and walnut one. That's amazing!

Steve: And what about drinks?

Hannah: The usual: orange juice, apple juice, tea, coffee or hot chocolate.

Steve: Wow! You really do know this place well. How can you remember all that?

Hannah: Easy. It's all on the menu up there, on the wall behind.

Lesson 7　Practice of disyllables
双音节拼读练习

Ⅰ. Related notions 相关概念

1. Syllable 音节

A syllable is a unit of significant sound formed by a vowel (e. g. a [eɪ], I [aɪ]) or a/some vowel(s) and a/some consonant(s) (e. g. in [ɪn], at [æt], me [miː], do [duː], hit [hɪt], speak [spiːk]). Generally, the number of syllables is related to the number of vowels, for example, no, win-dow, yes-ter-day etc.

音节是以元音音素为主体构成的发音单位,元音音素可以独自成音节,如 a [eɪ], I [aɪ]等,也可以与辅音结合构成音节,如 in[ɪn], at [æt], me[miː], do [duː], hit[hɪt], speak [spiːk]。一般来说,一个单词中有几个发音的元音字母,就有几个音节,如 no, win-dow, yes-ter-day 等。

Note:1) The silent "e" can't form a syllable. E. g. bike [baɪk], take [teɪk], etc.

2) Two or more vowels can be put together to form one significant sound, correspondingly, these vowels form only one syllable. E. g. book [bʊk], rain [reɪn], beau-ty[ˈbjuːti], etc.

3) Sometimes letters "le" can be connected with the consonant in front of them and make one syllable. E. g. ta-ble [ˈteɪbl], peo-ple [ˈpiːpl], etc.

注意:1) 单词末尾不发音的 e 不构成音节,如 bike [baɪk], take [teɪk]等。

2) 两个及以上元音字母在一起组成字母组合,发一个元音,构成一个音节,如 book [bʊk],rain [reɪn],beau-ty [ˈbjuːti] 等。

3) 词尾的 -le 可以和其前边的辅音组成一个音节,如 ta-ble [ˈteɪbl],peo-ple [ˈpiːpl] 等。

2. Stress 重音

If a word consists of two or more syllables, one of them is uttered more strongly or with longer sound, then this syllable is called a stressed syllable. Use "ˈ" to mark a stressed syllable (e. g volleyball [ˈvɒlɪbɔːl]). Sometimes a word contains both a primary stress and a secondary stress; use "ˌ" to mark the secondary stress (e. g. examination [ɪɡˌzæmɪˈneɪʃn]), which is stronger than a weak syllable, and weaker than a stressed one.

英语单词如果由两个及两个以上音节组成,其中有一个音节要读得更重、更响亮、更长,该音节被称为重读音节,在音标中用重音符号"ˈ"在该音节的左上角标示,如 volleyball [ˈvɒlɪbɔːl]。如果一个单词有多个音节,则除主重音外还有次重音,在左下角用"ˌ"标示,如 examination [ɪɡˌzæmɪˈneɪʃn]。

3. Disyllabic words 双音节词

Words that contain two syllables are disyllabic words, e. g. dri-ver, pil-low, etc.

含有两个音节的单词叫作双音节词,如 dri-ver, pil-low 等。

4. Polysyllabic words 多音节词

Words that contain three or more syllables are polysyllabic words, e. g. ham-bur-ger, un-im-por-tant, etc.

有三个或三个以上音节的词称为多音节词,如 ham-bur-ger, un-im-por-tant 等。

5. How to divide a word into syllables 如何划分音节

1) If there is one consonant between two vowels, distribute it to the latter

Lesson 7　Practice of disyllables 双音节拼读练习

syllable, e. g. a-gain, pa-per, stu-dent, ze-ro, etc.

如果两个元音字母之间只有一个辅音字母，通常将这个辅音字母划分给后一个音节，如 a-gain, pa-per, stu-dent, ze-ro 等。

2) If there are two consonants between two vowels, each vowel takes one consonant to form a syllable, e. g. mem-ber, let-ter, etc. If two consonants produce a consonant cluster, do not divide them up, e. g. fa-ther, tea-cher, be-tray. In addition, a consonant can constitute a syllable with sounds[l] [m] [n] behind it, so this consonant should be regarded as a part of the syllable with [l] [m] [n], e. g. ta-ble, pos-si-ble, ca-mel, so-cia-li-sm, sud-den, etc.

如果两个元音字母之间有两个辅音字母，则一个在前，一个在后，如 mem-ber, let-ter 等；但是如果两个相连的辅音字母是辅音连缀，则划分到后一个音节里，如 fa-ther,tea-cher,be-tray 等；另外，[l] [m] [n]可以与前面的辅音构成一个音节，此时要将该辅音字母与后面的[l] [m] [n]划分为一个音节，如 ta-ble, pos-si-ble, ca-mel, so-cia-li-sm, sud-den。

3) Vowels like *ea*, *ee*, *oo*, *er*, *ar*, *or*, *ur*, *ear*, *ure*, *ire*, *ore*, *are* make only one sound, do not divide them up, e. g. fur-ther, un-der-stood, etc.

元音字母组合如 ea, ee, oo, er, ar, or, ur, ear, ure, ire, ore, are 等只发一个音，划分音节时不可分开，如 fur-ther, un-der-stood 等。

4) Sometimes although two or more vowels are put together, they make sound independently, then divide them into different syllables, e. g. cre-ate [kriːˈeɪt],flu-ent [ˈfluːənt], etc.

如果两个元音并列，但不属于组合，则应分开划分音节，如：cre-ate [kriːˈeɪt], flu-ent [ˈfluːənt]等。

II. Phonetics for disyllables 双音节词的拼读

1. For most disyllables, the stress falls on the first syllable. 双音节词的重音大多在第一个音节上。

   after ['ɑːftə(r)]   always ['ɔːlweɪz]   April ['eɪprəl]
   bookcase ['bʊkkeɪs]   boring ['bɔːrɪŋ]   breakfast ['brekfəst]
   cousin ['kʌzn]   chicken ['tʃɪkɪn]   classmate ['klɑːsmeɪt]
   daughter ['dɔːtə(r)]   dinner ['dɪnə(r)]   dollar ['dɒlə(r)]
   easy ['iːzi]   e-mail ['iːmeɪl]   evening ['iːvnɪŋ]
   father ['fɑːðə(r)]   finish ['fɪnɪʃ]   grandma ['grænmɑː]
   habit ['hæbɪt]   healthy ['helθi]   history ['hɪstri]
   jacket ['dʒækɪt]   lesson ['lesn]   middle ['mɪdl]
   Monday ['mʌndeɪ]   morning ['mɔːnɪŋ]   notebook ['nəʊtbʊk]
   number ['nʌmbə(r)]   photo ['fəʊtəʊ]   picture ['pɪktʃə(r)]
   question ['kwestʃən]   radio ['reɪdiəʊ]   ruler ['ruːlə(r)]
   salad ['sæləd]   second ['sekənd]   sweater ['swetə(r)]
   table ['teɪbl]   thirty ['θɜːti]   tidy ['taɪdi]
   under ['ʌndə(r)]   useful ['juːsfl]   welcome ['welkəm]

2. For a small amount of disyllables, the stress falls on the second syllable. 小部分双音节词的重音在第二个音节上。

   about [ə'baʊt]   across [ə'krɒs]   ago [ə'gəʊ]
   because [bɪ'kɒz]   before [bɪ'fɔː]   between [bɪ'twiːn]
   enjoy [ɪn'dʒɔɪ]   forget [fə'get]   giraffe [dʒə'rɑːf]
   guitar [gɪ'tɑː]   hello [hə'ləʊ]   hotel [həʊ'tel]
   idea [aɪ'dɪə]   July [dʒu'laɪ]   police [pə'liːs]
   relax [rɪ'læks]   surprise [sə'praɪz]   today [tə'deɪ]

tonight [təˈnaɪt]   polite [pəˈlaɪt]   receive [rɪˈsiːv]

3. Thes tress in some words is changed according to their part of speech. Generally speaking, when a word is used as a noun, stress the first syllable; when it is a verb, stress the second syllable. 词性对双音节词重音的影响：一些双音节词在作名词和动词时重读音节不同。一般来说，作名词时，重读音节在前，作动词时，重读音节在后。

名 词		动 词	
the increase	[ˈɪnkriːs]	to increase	[ɪnˈkriːs]
the record	[ˈrekɔːd]	to record	[rɪˈkɔːd]
the object	[ˈɒbdʒɪkt]	to object	[əbˈdʒekt]
the subject	[ˈsʌbdʒɪkt]	to subject	[səbˈdʒekt]
the progress	[ˈprəʊgres]	to progress	[prəˈgres]
the desert	[ˈdezət]	to desert	[dɪˈzɜːt]
the present	[ˈpreznt]	to present	[prɪˈzent]
the produce	[ˈprɒdjuːs]	to produce	[prəˈdjuːs]
the transport	[ˈtrænspɔːt]	to transport	[trænˈspɔːt]

III. Practice 练习

1. Stress the first syllable 重读第一个音节

actor [ˈæktə(r)]   also [ˈɔːlsəʊ]   answer [ˈɑːnsə(r)]
boring [ˈbɔːrɪŋ]   baseball [ˈbeɪsbɔːl]   breakfast [ˈbrekfəst]
candle [ˈkændl]   center [ˈsentə(r)]   country [ˈkʌntri]
curly [ˈkɜːli]   dirty [ˈdɜːti]   dragon [ˈdrægən]
either [ˈaɪðə(r)]   fifty [ˈfɪfti]   follow [ˈfɒləʊ]
forest [ˈfɒrɪst]   funny [ˈfʌni]   hallway [ˈhɔːlweɪ]

handsome [ˈhænsəm]   heavy [ˈhevi]   hundred [ˈhʌndrəd]
into [ˈɪntə]   India [ˈɪndɪə]   kitchen [ˈkɪtʃɪn]
later [ˈleɪtə(r)]   lazy [ˈleɪzi]   listen [ˈlɪsn]
lucky [ˈlʌki]   medium [ˈmiːdɪəm]   minute [ˈmɪnɪt]
mountain [ˈmaʊntən]   noisy [ˈnɔɪzi]   practice [ˈpræktɪs]
problem [ˈprɒbləm]   quarter [ˈkwɔːtə(r)] robot [ˈrəʊbɒt]
Russian [ˈrʌʃn]   special [ˈspeʃl]   station [ˈsteɪʃn]
subway [ˈsʌbweɪ]   symbol [ˈsɪmbl]   visit [ˈvɪzɪt]
weather [ˈweðə(r)]   worry [ˈwʌri]

（以上例词选自人教版英语七年级下册）

2. Stress the second syllable 重读第二个音节

afraid [əˈfreɪd]   again [əˈgeɪn]   accept [əkˈsept]
become [bɪˈkʌm]   behind [bɪˈhaɪnd]   believe [bɪˈliːv]
cartoon [kɑːˈtuːn]   decide [dɪˈsaɪd]   delete [dɪˈliːt]
enough [ɪˈnʌf]   event [ɪˈvent]   exam [ɪgˈzæm]
himself [hɪmˈself]   improve [ɪmˈpruːv]   machine [məˈʃiːn]
percent [pəˈsent]   pollute [pəˈluːt]   refuse [rɪˈfjuːz]
result [rɪˈzʌlt]   surprised [səˈpraɪzd] unless [ənˈles]
yourself [jɔːˈself]

（以上例词选自人教版英语八年级上册）

Ⅳ. Additional practice 附加练习

1. Stress the first syllable 重读第一个音节

able [ˈeɪbl]   army [ˈɑːmi]   autumn [ˈɔːtəm]
better [ˈbetə(r)]   blender [ˈblendə(r)] butter [ˈbʌtə(r)]
common [ˈkɒmən]   concert [ˈkɒnsət]   crowded [ˈkraʊdɪd]

dentist ['dentɪst]   doctor ['dɒktə(r)]   expert ['ekspɜːt]
famous ['feɪməs]   foreign ['fɒrən]   future ['fjuːtʃə(r)]
happen ['hæpən]   hobby ['hɒbi]   human ['hjuːmən]
maybe ['meɪbi]   meaning ['miːnɪŋ]   mirror ['mɪrə(r)]
normal ['nɔːml]   paper ['peɪpə(r)]   pilot ['paɪlət]
program ['prəʊɡræm]   promise ['prɒmɪs]   ready ['redi]
reason ['riːzn]   rocket ['rɒkɪt]   service ['sɜːvɪs]
simple ['sɪmpl]   sitcom ['sɪtkɒm]   talent ['tælənt]
trader ['treɪdə(r)]   travel ['trævl]   video ['vɪdiəʊ]
wallet ['wɒlɪt]   wonder ['wʌndə(r)]   yogurt ['jɒɡət]

2. Stress the second syllable 重读第二个音节

advise [əd'vaɪz]   agree [ə'ɡriː]   although [ɔːl'ðəʊ]
appear [ə'pɪə(r)]   below [bɪ'ləʊ]   correct [kə'rekt]
collect [kə'lekt]   discuss [dɪ'skʌs]   dislike [dɪs'laɪk]
expect [ɪk'spekt]   invite [ɪn'vaɪt]   suggest [sə'dʒest]
mistake [mɪ'steɪk]   prepare [prɪ'peə(r)]   reply [rɪ'plaɪ]
success [sək'ses]   until [ən'tɪl]

Lesson 7   Homework

Ⅰ. 跟读模仿以下单词发音，按要求提交模仿作业。

village ['vɪlɪdʒ]   forget [fə'ɡet]   many ['meni]
behind [bɪ'haɪnd]   idea [aɪ'dɪə]   quiet ['kwaɪət]
afraid [ə'freɪd]   candy ['kændi]   tonight [tə'naɪt]
vacation [veɪ'keɪʃn]   subway ['sʌbweɪ]   enjoy [ɪn'dʒɔɪ]
painting ['peɪntɪŋ]   noisy ['nɔɪzi]   outside [ˌaʊt'saɪd]

weekend [ˌwiːkˈend] river [ˈrɪvə(r)] today [təˈdeɪ]
violin [ˌvaɪəˈlɪn] believe [bɪˈliːv]

Ⅱ. 跟读模仿下列对话，按要求提交模仿作业。

Conversation 1

A: Do you need any help?

B: Hi. These trousers—can I try them on, please?

A: Sure. What size do you take?

B: Not sure. 28 or 30.

A: And do you want them in red? We've got other colours, too.

B: Yes, I saw them, but it's the red ones I'm interested in.

A: No problem. So why don't you try both sizes? The changing rooms are in the corner.

B: Thanks!

Conversation 2

A: Can I help you?

B: Yeah. These football socks. How much are they? I can't find the price.

A: Just a moment. They're $8.99.

B: Fine. I'll take them.

A: OK, is that cash or card?

B: Cash.

A: That's great and here's your change and receipt.

B: Thanks.

Lesson 8　Practice of polysyllables
多音节拼读练习

Ⅰ. Related notion 相关概念

Polysyllables 多音节词

　　Words that contain three or more syllables are called polysyllables.
　　包含三个或三个音节以上的词称为多音节词。

Ⅱ. The stress in polysyllables 多音节词的重读

1. Usually the antepenult of a polysyllabic word is stressed; some words contain a secondary stress, which falls on the second syllable in front of the antepenult.

   多音节词的重音一般在倒数第三个音节上,再往前数的第二个音节一般还有次重音。

   American [əˈmerɪkən]　　activity [ækˈtɪvəti]　　basketball [ˈbɑːskɪtbɔːl]
   dictionary [ˈdɪkʃən(ə)ri]　difficult [ˈdɪfɪkəlt]　family [ˈfæməli]
   favorite [ˈfeɪvərɪt]　　festival [ˈfestəvl]　　grandfather [ˈɡrænfɑːðə]
   geography [dʒɪˈɒɡrəfi]　hamburger [ˈhæmbɜːɡə(r)]　interesting [ˈɪntrəstɪŋ]
   January [ˈdʒænjuəri]　　library [ˈlaɪbrəri]　　Saturday [ˈsætədeɪ]
   strawberry [ˈstrɔːbəri]　telephone [ˈtelɪfəun]　volleyball [ˈvɒlɪbɔːl]
   responsibility [rɪˌspɒnsəˈbɪləti]

2. **For words with some suffixes, stress the last syllable of the etyma.**
对于一些加后缀而来的派生词, 经常重读词干的最后一个音节。

-ion	educate [ˈedʒukeɪt]	education [ˌedʒuˈkeɪʃn]
	celebrate [ˈselɪbreɪt]	celebration [ˌselɪˈbreɪʃn]
	compete [kəmˈpiːt]	competition [ˌkɒmpəˈtɪʃn]
	repeat [rɪˈpiːt]	repetition [ˌrepəˈtɪʃn]
	expect [ɪkˈspekt]	expectation [ˌekspekˈteɪʃn]
	invite [ɪnˈvaɪt]	invitation [ˌɪnvɪˈteɪʃn]
	predict [prɪˈdɪkt]	prediction [prɪˈdɪkʃn]
-ity	active [ˈæktɪv]	activity [ækˈtɪvəti]
	disable [dɪsˈeɪbl]	disability [ˌdɪsəˈbɪləti]
	national [ˈnæʃnəl]	nationality [ˌnæʃəˈnæləti]
	possible [ˈpɒsəbl]	possibility [ˌpɒsəˈbɪləti]
	popular [ˈpɒpjələ(r)]	popularity [ˌpɒpjuˈlærəti]
-al	government [ˈɡʌvənmənt]	governmental [ˌɡʌvənˈmentl]
	development [dɪˈveləpmənt]	developmental [dɪˌveləpˈmentl]
-ic	hero [ˈhɪərəʊ]	heroic [hɪˈrəʊɪk]
	atom [ˈætəm]	atomic [əˈtɒmɪk]

Ⅲ. Practice 练习

Africa [ˈæfrɪkə]   anyone [ˈeniwʌn]

animal [ˈænɪml]   anything [ˈeniθɪŋ]

badminton [ˈbædmɪntən]   beautiful [ˈbjuːtɪfl]

butterfly [ˈbʌtəflaɪ]   Canada [ˈkænədə]

cinema [ˈsɪnəmə]   countryside [ˈkʌntrisaɪd]

elephant [ˈelɪfənt]   excellent [ˈeksələnt]

exercise [ˈeksəsaɪz]
hospital [ˈhɒspɪtl]
interested [ˈɪntrəstɪd]
uniform [ˈjuːnɪfɔːm]

neighborhood [ˈneɪbəhʊd]
holiday [ˈhɒlədeɪ]
natural [ˈnætʃərəl]
yesterday [ˈjestədeɪ]

Ⅳ. Additional practice 附加练习

article [ˈɑːtɪkl]
believable [bɪˈliːvəbl]
camera [ˈkæmərə]
congratulate [kənˈgrætʃʊleɪt]
capital [ˈkæpɪtl]
certainly [ˈsɜːtnli]
enemy [ˈenəmi]
excellent [ˈeksələnt]
finally [ˈfaɪnəli]
February [ˈfebrʊəri]
gentleman [ˈdʒentlmən]
instrument [ˈɪnstrəmənt]
medalist [ˈmedəlɪst]
manager [ˈmænɪdʒə(r)]
probably [ˈprɒbəbli]
relationship [rɪˈleɪʃnʃɪp]
restaurant [ˈrestrɒnt]
similar [ˈsɪmɪlə(r)]
technology [tekˈnɒlədʒi]
university [ˌjuːnɪˈvɜːsəti]

accident [ˈæksɪdənt]
calendar [ˈkælɪndə(r)]
communicate [kəˈmjuːnɪkeɪt]
character [ˈkærəktə(r)]
celebrate [ˈselɪbreɪt]
development [dɪˈveləpmənt]
economy [ɪˈkɒnəmi]
especially [ɪˈspeʃəli]
favourite [ˈfeɪvərɪt]
government [ˈgʌvənmənt]
impossibility [ɪmˌpɒsəˈbɪləti]
medical [ˈmedɪkl]
memory [ˈmeməri]
organize [ˈɔːgənaɪz]
possible [ˈpɒsəbl]
relative [ˈrelətɪv]
regular [ˈregjʊlə(r)]
stomachache [ˈstʌməkeɪk]
traditional [trəˈdɪʃənl]
wonderful [ˈwʌndəfl]

Lesson 8　Homework

Ⅰ. 跟读模仿以下单词发音,按要求提交模仿作业。

supermarket [ˈsuːpəmɑːkɪt]　　expensive [ɪkˈspensɪv]
anything [ˈeniθɪŋ]　　America [əˈmerɪkə]
England [ˈɪŋglənd]　　American [əˈmerɪkən]
everyone [ˈevriwʌn]　　policeman [pəˈliːsmən]
manager [ˈmænɪdʒə(r)]　　computer [kəmˈpjuːtə(r)]
furniture [ˈfɜːnɪtʃə(r)]　　television [ˈtelɪvɪʒn]
vegetable [ˈvedʒtəbl]　　library [ˈlaɪbrəri]
chocolate [ˈtʃɒklət]　　tomato [təˈmɑːtəʊ]
potato [pəˈteɪtəʊ]　　delicious [dɪˈlɪʃəs]
hamburger [ˈhæmbɜːgə(r)]　　banana [bəˈnɑːnə]
geography [dʒɪˈɒgrəfi]　　difficult [ˈdɪfɪkəlt]
interesting [ˈɪntrəstɪŋ]　　dangerous [ˈdeɪndʒərəs]

Ⅱ. 跟读模仿下列对话,按要求提交模仿作业。

DJ: So today we have a question for listeners, and it is: what's your favourite room, and why? Our first caller is... Hello, what's your name?

Jo: Hi there! My name's Jo.

DJ: OK Jo, so tell us, what's your favourite room?

Jo: It's my grandfather's playroom.

DJ: Your grandfather's got a playroom? Really?

Jo: Yeah. It's the room with his model trains. My grandad still lives in the house he lived in when he was a boy. And he has a little room with his trains. I love looking at his trains.

DJ: OK. And why is it special for you?

Jo: Because he's so happy there, and we sit and talk, and I feel very relaxed. It's lovely.

DJ: It sounds great.

Jo: Thank you.

Lesson 9 Mixed practice of monosyllables, disyllables and polysyllables
单音节、双音节、多音节混合拼读练习

I. Read the following words and split them into syllables
朗读下列单词,并划出下列单词的音节

(一)

apple [ˈæpl]	make [meɪk]	listen [ˈlɪsn]
forty [ˈfɔːti]	out [aʊt]	station [ˈsteɪʃn]
radio [ˈreɪdɪəʊ]	street [striːt]	luck [lʌk]
face [feɪs]	lion [ˈlaɪən]	cute [kjuːt]
fight [faɪt]	keep [kiːp]	heavy [ˈhevi]
soup [suːp]	wear [weə(r)]	box [bɒks]
true [truː]	skate [skeɪt]	year [jɪə(r)]
noisy [ˈnɒɪzi]	sorry [ˈsɒri]	ivory [ˈaɪvəri]
race [reɪs]	scary [ˈskeəri]	police [pəˈliːs]
strict [strɪkt]	height [haɪt]	actress [ˈæktrəs]
sunny [ˈsʌni]	student [ˈstjuːdnt]	

(二)

hair [heə(r)]	pencil [ˈpensl]	model [ˈmɒdl]
favorite [ˈfeɪvərɪt]	often [ˈɒfn]	eraser [ɪˈreɪzə(r)]

Lesson 9 Mixed practice of monosyllables, disyllables and polysyllables
单音节、双音节、多音节混合拼读练习

candle ['kændl]
either ['aɪðə(r)]
sale [seɪl]
medium ['miːdiəm]
winter ['wɪntə(r)]
follow ['fɒləʊ]
ring [rɪŋ]
vacation [veɪ'keɪʃn]
flower ['flaʊə(r)]
violin [ˌvaɪə'lɪn]
July [dʒʊ'laɪ]
geography [dʒɪ'ɒgrəfi]
twelfth [twelfθ]
picture ['pɪktʃə(r)]
again [ə'gen]
restaurant ['restrɒnt]
thirteen [θɜː'tiːn]
lesson ['lesn]
horse [hɔːs]
ice-cream [aɪs'kriːm]
daughter ['dɔːtə(r)]
porridge ['pɒrɪdʒ]
head [hed]
Saturday ['sætədeɪ]
message ['mesɪdʒ]
newspaper ['njuːzpeɪpə(r)]

interesting ['ɪntrəstɪŋ]
guitar [gɪ'tɑː]
hotel [həʊ'tel]
habit ['hæbɪt]
subject ['sʌbdʒɪkt]
cinema ['sɪnəmə]
carrot ['kærət]
late [leɪt]
Tuesday ['tjuːzdeɪ]
because [bɪ'kɒz]
animal ['ænɪml]
about [ə'baʊt]
important [ɪm'pɔːtnt]
science ['saɪəns]
quickly ['kwɪkli]
color ['kʌlə(r)]
weekend [ˌwiːk'end]
practice ['præktɪs]
hospital ['hɒspɪtl]
small [smɔːl]
between [bɪ'twiːn]
delicious [dɪ'lɪʃəs]
koala [kəʊ'ɑːlə]
little ['lɪtl]
elephant ['elɪfənt]
supermarket ['suːpəmɑːkɪt]

study ['stʌdi]
uniform ['juːnɪfɔːm]
thirty ['θɜːti]
afraid [ə'freɪd]
pick [pɪk]
ropeway ['rəʊpˌweɪ]
weather ['weðə(r)]
happy ['hæpi]
only ['əʊnli]
dictionary ['dɪkʃənri]
festival ['festɪvl]
movie ['muːvi]
white [waɪt]
remember [rɪ'membə(r)]
popular ['pɒpjʊlə(r)]
terrible ['terəbl]
near [nɪə(r)]
beautiful ['bjuːtɪfl]
Chinese [tʃaɪ'niːz]
minute ['mɪnɪt]
blue [bluː]
tomorrow [tə'mɒrəʊ]
birthday ['bɜːθdeɪ]
dragon ['drægən]
bridge [brɪdʒ]

Ⅱ. Additional practice 附加练习

late [leɪt]　　　　　　ninety [ˈnaɪnti]　　　　　　teacher [ˈtiːtʃə(r)]
exercise [ˈeksəsaɪz]　　curly [ˈkɜːli]　　　　　　symbol [ˈsɪmbl]
person [ˈpɜːsn]　　　　breakfast [ˈbrekfəst]　　　table [ˈteɪbl]
center [ˈsentə(r)]　　　village [ˈvɪlɪdʒ]　　　　　February [ˈfebruəri]
write [raɪt]　　　　　　mutton [ˈmʌtn]　　　　　　chicken [ˈtʃɪkɪn]
delicious [dɪˈlɪʃəs]　　　come [kʌm]　　　　　　　piano [pɪˈænəʊ]
giraffe [dʒəˈrɑːf]　　　basketball [ˈbɑːskɪtbɔːl]　　air [eə(r)]
money [ˈmʌni]　　　　healthy [ˈhelθi]　　　　　　mountain [ˈmaʊntən]
warm [wɔːm]　　　　　office [ˈɒfɪs]　　　　　　　father [ˈfɑːðə(r)]
excellent [ˈeksələnt]　　like [laɪk]　　　　　　　　feed [fiːd]
straight [streɪt]　　　　December [dɪˈsembə(r)]　　fire [ˈfaɪə(r)]
pool [puːl]　　　　　　young [jʌŋ]　　　　　　　exciting [ɪkˈsaɪtɪŋ]
brush [brʌʃ]　　　　　house [haʊs]　　　　　　　Canada [ˈkænədə]
museum [mjʊˈzɪəm]　　town [taʊn]　　　　　　　listen [ˈlɪsn]
practice [ˈpræktɪs]　　　expensive [ɪkˈspensɪv]　　　street [striːt]
koala [kəʊˈɑːlə]　　　　twentieth [ˈtwentɪəθ]　　　Europe [ˈjʊərəp]
usually [ˈjuːʒuəli]　　　grandmother [ˈgrænmʌðə(r)]　special [ˈspeʃəl]
excuse [ɪkˈskjuːz]

Lesson 9　Homework

Ⅰ. 跟读模仿以下单词发音，按要求提交模仿作业。

Chinese [ˌtʃaɪˈniːz]　　from [frɒm; frəm]　　where [weə(r)]
about [əˈbaʊt]　　　　our [ˈaʊə(r)]　　　　　grade [greɪd]
China [ˈtʃaɪnə]　　　　very [ˈveri]　　　　　　city [ˈsɪti]

Lesson 9 Mixed practice of monosyllables, disyllables and polysyllables
单音节、双音节、多音节混合拼读练习

first [fɜːst]	small [smɔːl]	last [lɑːst]
aunt [ɑːnt; ænt]	brother [ˈbrʌðə(r)]	cousin [ˈkʌzən]
daughter [ˈdɔːtə(r)]	son [sʌn]	photo [ˈfəʊtəʊ]
these [ðiːz]	uncle [ˈʌŋkl]	hotel [həʊˈtel]
they [ðeɪ]	left [left]	right [raɪt]
woman [ˈwʊmən]	front [frʌnt]	those [ðəʊz]
station [ˈsteɪʃ(ə)n]	theatre [ˈθɪətə(r)]	actor [ˈæktə(r)]
driver [ˈdraɪvə(r)]	job [dʒɒb]	doctor [ˈdɒktə(r)]
manager [ˈmænɪdʒə(r)]	nurse [nɜːs]	their [ðeə(r)]
document [ˈdɒkjumənt]	company [ˈkʌmpəni]	Australia [ɒsˈtreɪlɪə]
customer [ˈkʌstəmə(r)]	holiday [ˈhɒlədeɪ]	information [ˌɪnfəˈmeɪʃn]

Ⅱ. 跟读模仿下列对话，按要求提交模仿作业。

DJ: What's your name and what's your favourite room?

Andrew: Hi. I'm Andrew and my favourite room is the music room at my school.

DJ: OK, Andrew. And why's that?

Andrew: It's because I love playing the drums, but I can't have drums at home, so I go into the music room at school and practise there. After school, no one cares. I have a lot of fun!

DJ: Sounds good to me! Thanks, Andrew. Next caller please! Hello!

Paula: Hello, I'm Paula. My favourite room is our kitchen at home. I love it there because that's where all of us sit and have our breakfast and dinner, and we're a family together. It makes me feel really nice and warm.

DJ: Nice and warm. That's a good reason.

Paula: Yeah, and kind of ... I don't know, safe.

DJ: Excellent, Paula, thank you.

Lesson 10　Stress, liaison and loss of plosion
　　　　　重读,连读,失去爆破

Ⅰ. Some interesting pronunciation phenomena 有趣的发音现象

1. Sentence stress 句子重音

　　当我们和母语为英语的人交谈时,发现他们并不是每一个单词都读得一样响亮、清楚。有些单词读起来又轻又快,而且较为含糊,而有些单词读得又重又慢,而且十分清晰。这是为什么呢？原来,在连贯的话语中,不可能所有的单词都同样重要,也不可能把时间平均分配给每一个词,否则就会令听者觉得说话人轻重不分,主次不明。一般来说,在句子中需重读的多为实词,如名词、动词、形容词、副词、数词等。不需重读的多为虚词,如冠词、连词、介词等。句子重音更能体现出句子的节奏和韵律感,同时能突出重点,使听者更加容易理解。

　　1) Stress and reduction 重读和弱读

　　哪些单词或音节需重读,这取决于说话人想要强调什么。然而,一个句子中哪些词需要重读,哪些词需要轻读,还是有规可循的。通常我们把词分为实义词(实词)和功能词(虚词)。实义词指本身具有意义的词,而功能词主要指本身基本没有意义,但是起到语法作用的词。因此,英语语句中的实义词,往往重读,重读音节须长而响亮,这便形成了句子重音;功能词在句中一般弱读。

　　实义词包括名词、实义动词、形容词、副词、数量词、指示代词、疑问代词、物主代词、否定词和感叹词等。

　　虚词包括冠词、介词、连词、助动词、关系代词等。如：

　　a. 'When is 'your 'birthday?

　　b. I 'don't 'like to 'get 'up 'early.

Lesson 10 Stress, liaison and loss of plosion 重读，连读，失去爆破

c. They're 'two 'dollars.

d. 'What's 'this in 'English?

e. 'Spell it, 'please.

f. Did you 'have a 'good 'weekend?

当然，我们也可以根据说话人的意图，"重读"一个或多个本应该"非重读"的词，这便是由具体语境决定的逻辑重音。

例如，一般情况下，"I can help you."这句话，只有 help 需重读，但若想表达不同的意图，可按不同需要重读不同的单词，试比较下面三句话的不同含义：

a. 'I can help you. 我会帮助你的。（意思是，别人帮不了你）

b. I 'can help you. 我会帮助你的。（意思是，别以为我帮不了你）

c. I can help 'you. 我会帮助你。（意思是，我会帮你，别人我不帮。）

试练习：

a. —This is 'my book.

—Oh no, it 'isn't. It's my book.

b. —Would you like a large bowl?

—No, I'd like a 'small bowl.

另外，通常情况下实义词需要重读，但也并非时时处处都重读。例如：

a. —What's her 'name?

—Her name's Jane.

b. —When is your 'birthday, Linda?

—My birthday is on May 2nd.

这两个例子中，name 和 birthday 在问句中都是重读词，但是在答句中，不属于强调内容，因此都可非重读。

试练习：（同一句子"He is watering flowers."，不同重音读法）

a. —What is he doing?

—He is 'watering 'flowers.

b. —Is he watering grass?

—'No, he is watering 'flowers.

c. —Is he planting flowers?

—'No, he is 'watering flowers.

d. —Is she watering flowers?

—'No, 'he is watering flowers.

2) Strong forms and weak forms 强读式和弱读式

在句子里,有语句重音的词在读音上需采用强读形式(strong form),即单词的词典发音;没有语句重音的词,应采用其弱读形式(weak form)。虽然一般虚词是弱读式读音,但这里也列举了其强读式(即字典发音)。列表如下:

词类		强 读	弱 读
人称代词	you	[juː]	[jʊ], [jə]
	he	[hiː]	[i]
	she	[ʃiː]	[ʃi]
	we	[wiː]	[wi]
	me	[miː]	[mi]
	him	[hɪm]	[ɪm]
	us	[ʌs]	[əs], [s]
	her	[hɜː]	[hə], [ə]
	them	[ðem]	[ðəm], [əm]
物主代词	my	[maɪ]	[mɪ]
	your	[jɔː]	[jʊ], [jə]
	his	[hɪz]	[ɪz], [z]
	her	[hɜː]	[hə], [ə]
反身代词	myself	[maɪˈself]	[məˈself]
	yourself	[jɔːˈself]	[jəˈself]
	herself	[hɜːˈself]	[həˈself]
关系代词	who	[huː]	[hʊ]
	whom	[huːm]	[hʊm]
	whose	[huːz]	[hʊz]
	that	[ðæt]	[ðət]

续表

词类		强 读	弱 读
动词 be	be	[biː]	[bi]
	am	[ˈæm]	[əm], [m]
	are	[ɑː]	[ə]
	is	[ɪz]	[z], [s]
	was	[wɒz]	[wəz], [wz]
	were	[wɜː]	[wə]
助动词	have	[hæv]	[həv], [əv]
	has	[hæz]	[həz], [əz]
	had	[hæd]	[həd], [əd]
	do	[duː]	[də], [d]
	does	[dʌz]	[dəz]
	shall	[ʃæl]	[ʃəl]
	should	[ʃʊd]	[ʃəd]
	will	[wɪl]	[wəl], [l]
	would	[wʊd]	[wəd], [d]
	can	[kæn]	[kən], [kn]
	could	[kʊd]	[kəd], [kd]
	must	[mʌst]	[məst]
冠词	a	[eɪ]	[ə]
	an	[æn]	[ən]
	the	[ðiː]	[ðə](辅音前), [ði](元音前)
连词	and	[ænd]	[ənd], [ən]
	but	[bʌt]	[bət]
	than	[ðæn]	[ðən], [ðn]
	that	[ðæt]	[ðət]
	as	[æz]	[əz]
引导词	there	[ðeə]	[ðə]
副词	not	[nɒt]	[nt], [n]
其他词	some	[sʌm]	[səm]
	such	[sʌtʃ]	[sətʃ]

试练习:

a. Give **us some** more. ([əs] [səm])

b. Two nice photos **of** my family. ([əv])

c. I have my jacket **and** hat. ([ən])

d. I'm tidy, **but** Gina is not. ([bət])

e. I worked **as** a guide at the Natural History Museum. ([əz])

2. Liaison 连读

为了使语句听起来更顺畅,我们把同一意群(即短语或从句)中相邻单词的词尾和词首的两个音素粘连起来,形成新的音节,这就是连读。连读所构成的音节一般都不重读,只需要顺其自然地带过,不加音不重读。例如:

Put it on, please.

这个句子有两处连读。第一处是 put 的尾辅音[t]与 it 的开头元音[ɪ],连读为[tɪ],第二处是 it 的尾辅音[t]与 on 的开头元音[ɒ]连读为[tɒ]。"‿"为连读符号。

需要注意,连读只发生在同一意群当中。换言之,若在两个意群之间,即使满足连读条件,也不可以连读。如"Have a look at it.",因句子同属一个意群,所以可连读;而另一个句子"There is a map in it."中,map 和 in 虽满足连读条件,但因不同属一个意群,往往不连读。我们再看几个例子:

1) Not at all. (可以连读)

2) Have a good day!

3) Can I take a message for him.

4) Do you walk or ride a bike? (walk 和 or 不连读)

Liaison rules 连读规则

1) 词尾辅音+词首元音

例如:take it off   think about   kind of   get up   a lot of
      What about   Half an hour   walk out   eat out

2) 字母 r 或 re 结尾+词首元音

如果前一个词是以-r 或-re 结尾,后一个词是以元音开头,这时的 r 或 re 不但要发[r]，而且还要与后面的元音拼起来连读。

例如：for example   far away   after all   for ever

This is our own home.

Where is a will, there is a way.

3) 元音＋元音

如果前一个词以元音结尾，后一个词以元音开头，这两个音往往也要自然连读在一起。

a. 扁唇元音＋元音 ——连读时元音间要加入轻微[j]音

例如：Can you **see it**?   [si: jit]

扁唇元音有[i:] [ɪ] [eɪ] [aɪ] [ɔɪ]

试练习：

see off   stay up   lay out   be on time   play around

any other   try it   the other   I can't carry it.   the end

b. 圆唇元音＋元音 ——连读时元音间要加入轻微[w]音

例如：Do you **know it**?   [nəʊwɪt]

圆唇元音有[u:] [ʊ] [əʊ] [aʊ]

试练习：

go out   blow out   throw away   go outside   how old   how about

I saw it.   Do it now.   You are welcome.

3. Loss of Plosion 失去爆破

1) What is plosion? 什么是爆破音？

爆破音是指发音器官在口腔中形成阻碍，气流冲破阻碍发出的音。这类音有 6 个，分别为[p] [b] [t] [d] [k]和[g]。

2) Loss of plosion and partial loss of plosion 失去爆破和部分失去爆破

a. 两个爆破音相邻，前一个爆破音，只作发音的姿势，稍作停留但不发出音，这样的发音过程，叫作失去爆破。例如，book<u>c</u>ase, basket<u>b</u>all 等。

b. <u>当一个爆破音和其他辅音相邻</u>，发此爆破音时，发音器官不形成阻碍只形成狭小缝隙，气流从其流出，这种不完全的爆破的发音过程，叫作部分失去爆破。

例如,thanks,breakfast 等。

3) Rules of loss of plosion and partial loss of plosion 失去爆破和部分失去爆破的规则

a.（失去爆破）　爆破音＋爆破音

例如：actor　doctor　September　October　cut down

I have a bad cold today.　What time is it now?

b.（不完全失去爆破）　爆破音＋摩擦音/破擦音

摩擦音 10 个：[f] [v] [θ] [ð] [s] [z] [ʃ] [ʒ] [r] [h]

破擦音 6 个：[ts] [dz] [tr] [dr] [tʃ] [dʒ]

此部分爆破音部分失去爆破,只能听到轻微的爆破声,主要听到的是后面的摩擦音或破擦音。

例如：picture　handsome　outside　read the book

get dressed　take the subway　Please help them!

c.（不完全失去爆破）　爆破音＋鼻音

第一种情况：

爆破音[t] [d]紧跟鼻辅音[m] [n],组成一个音节时,爆破在鼻中实施,语音学叫鼻腔爆破。如 mutton ['mʌtn],written ['rɪtn]等。常见错误是在[tn] [dn]间错误地加入[ə],读成 [tən] [dən]。

例如：beaten　forgotten　certain　garden　pardon　widen　student

第二种情况：

爆破音[t] [d]在鼻辅音[m] [n]前面,分属不同音节,部分爆破,只能听到轻微爆破声,主要听到后面的鼻音。

例如：midnight　partner　Britain　Good morning, sir! Sorry, I don't know.

d.（不完全失去爆破）　爆破音＋舌侧音

第一种情况：

爆破音[t] [d]紧跟舌侧音[l],组成一个音节时,[t] [d]的爆破随[l]而出,语音学称为"舌侧爆破",如：little,middle,model,noodle,candle 等。这里要注意,发音和[təʊ] [dəʊ]区别开。

第二种情况：

爆破音[t][d]在舌侧音[l]前面，分属不同音节，部分爆破，只能听到轻微爆破声，主要听到后面的舌侧音。

例如：frien_dly　lou_dly　col_dly　I don't like it.

Lesson 10　Homework

Ⅰ. 跟读模仿以下句子发音，按要求提交模仿作业。

1. We're going to work on a farm nex(t) Tuesday.
2. What would you like, ho(t) tea or bla(ck) coffee?
3. It's a very col(d) day, but it's a goo(d) day.
4. You can put i(t) down in the bi(g) garden.
5. I bought a chea(p) book, but it's a goo(d) book.
6. I wan(t) to come but I can't.
7. He's rich and famous.
8. He's older than she is.
9. I bought a red handbag.
10. Tommy is a good book-keeper.

Ⅱ. 跟读模仿下列对话，按要求提交模仿作业。

Conversation 1

A: Hello. Can I help you?
B: Hi, yes. Where can I find toothbrushes?
A: They're just there on your right.
B: Oh yes. I didn't see them. OK, I'll take this one.

A: Is that all?

B: No, there's this toothpaste, too.

A: OK. So that's £4.30.

B: Here you are.

A: And that's 70p change. Have a nice day.

B: Thank you.

Conversation 2

A: Are you all right there?

B: Yes, thanks. I just want a cover for my new phone. Have you got this one in red?

A: Sorry, only black.

B: OK, black's fine. I'll take it.

A: Right. That's £12.99, please.

B: Can I pay with my contactless card?

A: Of course. Just place it over here.

B: OK.

A: Great. That's gone through. Would you like your receipt?

B: No, it's OK.

Lesson 11　Intonation of different types of sentences
不同类型的句子的语调

Ⅰ. Different intonation patterns 句子的不同语调类型

Intonation, the tone of speech, refers to the distribution and change of tone of pitch in a sentence. Intonation is an important means of nonverbal communication. Different intonations allow people to express different emotions, such as joy, sadness, curiosity, anger, doubt, etc. Broadly speaking, two basic intonations in English are the falling tone and the rising tone. Specially, English intonations fall into the following several patterns: the falling tone, the rising tone, the rising-falling tone, the falling-rising tone and the falling-falling tone.

语调,即说话的腔调,指一句话里声调的高低配置变化。语调是非言语交际的重要手段。不同的语调能使人表达不同的感情,如喜悦、悲伤、好奇、愤怒、疑问等。从广义上讲,英语中的两个基本语调是降调和升调。具体来说,英语句子的语调可分为以下几种:降调、升调、升降调、降升调及降降调。

1. The falling tone 降调

In sentences that need to be read in a falling tone, the first stressed syllable is read with the highest pitch of the speaking voice and those that follow are read in the pitch falling successively. The tone falls at the last stressed syllable.

在需要用降调的句子中,第一个重读音节的音最高,其后的音依次递降,语调在最后一个重读音节降下来。

The falling tone, meaning "completeness" and "certainty", is mainly used in general declarative sentences, imperative sentences expressing commands, exclamatory sentences, special questions, and yes-no questions expressing criticism, blame, etc.

在英语语调中,降调表示"完整"和"肯定",主要用于普通陈述句、表示命令的祈使句、感叹句、特殊疑问句、表批评或指责等的一般疑问句中。

1) General declarative sentences 普通陈述句

In general declarative sentences, the speaker is sure of what he says in both meaning and structure regardless of the positive or negative meaning of the sentence. The falling tone is usually used in these sentences. That is, the tone falls at the last notional word of the sentence. For example:

在普通陈述句中,不论含义的肯否,说话人对自己所表达的内容语气肯定,含义和结构完整,一般用降调,即在句子最后的一个实词处往下降。例如:

John likes ↘ salad.

Those are my ↘ parents.

There's a zoo in my ↘ neighborhood.

They are on the ↘ table.

My birthday is in ↘ August.

2) Imperative sentences expressing commands 表示命令的祈使句

The falling tone is used in imperative sentences that express strong commands in a serious tone. For example:

在表示强烈命令的祈使句中,说话人语气非常强硬,句末用降调。例如:

Get ↘ up.

Be ↘ quiet.

Clean the ↘ room.

Don't eat in ↘ class.

Let's see the pandas ↘ first.

3) Exclamatory sentences 感叹句

The falling tone is used in exclamatory sentences to express strong exclamations of praise, amazement, etc. For example:

感叹句用降调,表示说话人强烈的赞美、惊异等感叹语气。例如:

Oh ↘ great!

What a great ↘ day!

What ↘ fun!

How time ↘ flies!

How ↘ interesting!

4) Special questions 特殊疑问句

Special questions are sentences introduced by wh-words such as *what*, *when*, *why*, *where* and so on. The falling tone is used to express the strong interest of the speaker. For example:

以 what、when、why、where 等特殊疑问词引导的疑问句是特殊疑问句,一般在句尾用降调,表示说话人浓厚的兴趣。例如:

What did you do last ↘ weekend?

When do your friends ↘ exercise?

Why do you like ↘ pandas?

Where did you go on ↘ vacation?

How often do you eat ↘ fruit?

5) Yes-no questions expressing criticism, blame, etc. 表批评、指责等的一般疑问句。

In yes-no questions, if the speaker expresses dissatisfaction, impatience, criticism, blame and so on, the falling tone is usually used at the end of the sentence. Answers are not necessary in such sentences because they seem obvious. For example:

在一般疑问句中,若说话人对对方表示不满、没耐心、批评、指责等时,句末用降调。这类句子不需要回答,因为答案是显而易见的。例如:

① Will you be late ↘ again? (You shouldn't be late.)

② Is there anything else you want to ↘ say? (You have said enough.)

In example ①, the speaker is very dissatisfied with the other person's being late, so he asks if he will be late again. Clearly, the speaker doesn't think it suitable for the other person to be late. Although the yes-no question is used here, its meaning is very clear: the other person shouldn't be late again. Here, the falling tone is used.

在例①中,说话人对对方迟到这一行为表示非常不满,所以询问对方是否还会迟到。显然,说话人认为对方迟到是不合适的,虽然用的是一般疑问句,但表达的意思是很明确的:对方不应该再迟到了。此时用降调。

2. The rising tone 升调

In sentences that need to be read in a rising tone, the first stressed syllable is read with the highest pitch of the speaking voice and those that follow are read in the pitch falling successively. The tone rises at the last syllable.

在需要用升调的句子中,第一个重读音节的音最高,其后的音依次递降,语调在最后一个音节上上升。

In English intonation, the rising tone is used to express uncertainty, politeness, euphemism, requests and so on. It is often used in general yes-no questions, imperative sentences expressing requests, concern, etc., questions in the form of statements, greetings, special questions asking for repetition, expressing friendliness and concern and so on.

在英语语调中,我们用升调表达说话人的不肯定、礼貌、委婉、征求意见等意味。升调常用于普通的一般疑问句、表示请求和关心等的祈使句、陈述句形式的疑问句、问候语、请对方重复或表示友好和关切等的特殊疑问句中。

1) General yes-no questions 普通的一般疑问句

Usually, the rising tone is used in yes-no questions to express the doubt or uncertainty of the speaker. For example:

通常,一般疑问句用升调,表达说话人的疑问。例如:

Is this your ↗ pencil?

Do you have a ↗ baseball?

Are they using the ↗ computer?

May I take your ↗ order?

Lesson 11 Intonation of different types of sentences 不同类型的句子的语调

Would you like any ↗ drinks?

2) Imperative sentences expressing requests, concern, etc. 表示请求、关心等的祈使句

The rising tone is used in imperative sentences which express requests, concern, encouragement, indirect suggestions and so on. In this way the tone seems gentler and sounds more polite. For example:

当祈使句表示请求、关心、鼓励、不直接的建议等时用升调,这样语气会稍显柔和,听起来更有礼貌。例如:

No ↗ problem.

Good for ↗ you.

Come ↗ on.

Don't ↗ worry.

Take ↗ care.

3) Questions in the form of statements 陈述句形式的疑问句

Questions in the form of statements are made up of statements and question marks, expressing uncertainty, doubt, surprise, euphemism, comfort, encouragement and sometimes query or rebuttal. The rising tone should be used. For example:

陈述句形式的疑问句由陈述句加问号构成,表示说话人的不肯定、怀疑、惊讶、委婉、安慰、鼓励等感情,有时候表示质疑或反驳。此时应读成升调。例如:

And my ↗ hat?

You want to ↗ rest?

That is your ↗ pencil?

You ↗ did?

We're meeting at seven, ↗ right?

4) Greetings 问候语

Greetings are the expressions people use when they meet or say goodbye to others. The rising tone is often used. For example:

人们见面打招呼或离别时的用语称作问候语,一般用升调。例如:

Good ↗ afternoon.

Hello, ↗ Frank.

Have a good ↗ day.

Nice to meet ↗ you.

See you ↗ later.

5) Special questions asking for repetition, expressing friendliness and concern and so on 请对方重复或表示友好和关切等的特殊疑问句

The rising tone is used in special questions that ask for repetition or sometimes show mild criticism, friendliness or concern. For example:

特殊疑问句用升调表示说话者没听清楚,请对方再说一遍。有时也表示温和的批评或友好和关切。例如:

↗ What? （没听清,请对方再说一遍）

What did you ↗ do? （刚才没看清楚）

How much is ↗ it? （表示温和的批评,嫌弃价格太高）

What's your↗ name? （表示友好和关切）

In English, some sentences only adopt one intonation pattern, while some need two: the rising-falling tone, the falling-rising tone or the falling-falling tone.

英语中,有的句子只使用一种语调,有的句子需使用两种语调:升降调(先升后降),降升调(先降后升)或降降调(句子前后两部分都用降调)。

3．The rising-falling tone 升降调

The rising-falling tone is mainly used in the following types of sentences.

升降调主要用于下列句式中。

1) Alternative questions 选择疑问句

Generally, the rising tone is used in the first several options of alternative questions to express the incompleteness of the meaning, while the falling tone is used in the last option to show the end of the options. For example:

通常,在选择疑问句的若干选项中,前几个选项用升调,表示含义不完整,最后

一个选项用降调，表示选项结束。例如：

Do you go by ↗bus or by ↘ train?

Is he↗ tall or ↘ short?

Would you like some ↗ tea, ↗ coffee, or ↘ milk?

What color is it, ↗ red, ↗ blue or ↘ white?

Are you studying ↗ hard, or are you having ↘ fun?

2）Sentences with adverbial phrases or adverbial clauses being at the beginning 句首是状语短语或状语从句的句子

The rising tone is used in adverbial phrases or adverbial clauses that are at the beginning of a sentence to express the incompleteness of the meaning, while the falling tone is used in the main clause to show the completeness of the meaning. For example：

在以状语短语或状语从句开始的句子中，状语短语或状语从句部分用升调，表示含义不完整，主句用降调，表示含义完结。例如：

At the ↗ museum, I learned a lot about ↘ robots.

On the first ↗ night, we just sat under the ↘ moon.

Once upon a ↗ time, there was a very old ↘ man.

When I read ↗ books, time goes ↘ quickly.

To get ↗ there, I usually walk out and turn right on Bridge↘ Road.

3）Declarative sentences listing people or things 列举多项人或事物的陈述句

When several people or things are listed in declarative sentences, the rising tone is used in the first several items, while the falling tone is used in the last item to show the completion of the list. For example：

陈述句中列举人或事物时，前几个用升调，以区别语义，最后一个用降调，表列举完结。例如：

This is a photo of my family; these are my ↗ parents, my ↗ brothers, and this is my ↘ sister.

Gina's books are everywhere — on her ↗ bed, on the ↗ sofa and under the ↘ chair.

I have two soccer ↗balls, three ↗ volleyballs, four ↗ basketballs and five ↗ baseballs and the ↘ bats.

I'd like ↗chicken, ↗ potato, and cabbage ↘ noodles.

They try to look for the best ↗ singers, the most talented ↗ dancers, the most exciting ↗ magicians, the most funniest ↗ actors and so ↘on.

4．The falling-rising tone 降升调

The falling-rising tone is mainly used in the following types of sentences.
降升调主要用于下列句式中。

1) Disjunctive questions expressing uncertainty 对陈述部分不确定的反意疑问句

The falling tone is used in the declarative part of disjunctive questions. If the speaker is unsure of the declarative part, the rising tone is used in the tag questions to expect the affirmation of the other person. For example:

反意疑问句的陈述部分用降调,若说话者对陈述部分不确定,附加问句部分用升调,表示期待对方确认。例如:

You want to talk to ↘ her, ↗ don't you? （不确定对方是否想）

Can you ↘ swim, ↗ can't you?

It's hot in your ↘ country, ↗ isn't it?

The weather is ↘ great, ↗ isn't it?

School Day is on October ↘ 22nd, ↗ isn't it?

2) Declarative sentences followed by additional parts or adverbials expressed in an uncertain or hesitant tone 前面是陈述句,后面是语气不肯定或迟疑的附加语或状语

When additional parts or adverbials, placed at the end of the main clauses, are said in a hesitant tone or are temporarily added, the falling tone is used in the main clause and the rising tone is used in the additional or adverbial part. For example:

有的附加语或状语放在主句后面,说出来的口吻较为犹豫,或者是临时想起来

补充上去的,主句部分用降调,附加语或状语部分用升调。例如:

Larry is much less ↘ hard-working, ↗ though.

The weather here is cool and ↘ cloudy, just right for ↗ walking.

I'm going to keep on writing ↘ stories, of ↗ course.

We will certainly feel ↘ worse, unless we talk to ↗ someone.

Please let us ↘ know, if you can come to the ↗ party.

5. The falling-falling tone 降降调

The falling-falling tone is mainly used in the following types of sentences. 降降调主要用于下列句式中。

1) Disjunctive questions expressing certainty 对陈述部分把握较大的反意疑问句

Disjunctive questions consist of the declarative part and the tag question part. The falling tone is used in the declarative part. If the speaker is sure about what he expresses in the declarative part, the falling tone is also used in the question part. Such sentences usually express some certainty and don't need answers or affirmation of the other person. For example:

反意疑问句由陈述部分+附加疑问部分构成,陈述部分用降调,若说话者对陈述部分把握较大,后半部分也用降调。这样的句子一般不需要回答,有强烈的陈述意味,无须对方证实。例如:

It's hot in your country ↘ now, ↘ isn't it? (明知很热)

You want to talk to ↘ her, ↘ don't you? (很清楚对方的想法)

The weather is ↘ great, ↘ isn't it? (看到外面阳光明媚)

It's ↘ cold, ↘ isn't it? (天确实很冷)

That's ↘ Tara, ↘ isn't it? (明知是对方)

2) Declarative sentences with the main clauses followed by adverbials or adverbial clauses 状语或状语从句在主句之后的陈述句

In sentences with the main clauses followed by adverbials or adverbial clauses, the falling tone is usually used in the main clauses to express the completeness of the main information. What's more, the falling tone is also used in the adverbial parts. For example:

在主句在前,状语或状语从句在后的句子中,主句一般用降调,表示主要信息已表述完毕,状语部分也用降调。例如：

I like ↘ him because he is cool and ↘ fun.

The food tasted ↘ great because I was so ↘ hungry.

Our dog welcomed ↘ me when I came home from ↘ school.

You can put ↘ more if you ↘ like.

Game shows are the most ↘ popular although many students like to watch ↘ sports.

3) Coordinate sentences 并列句

There are usually conjunctions like *and*, *but*, *or* and so on to connect the two equivalents of coordinate sentences. The falling tone is usually used in both of the two clauses. For example:

并列句通常由连接词 and、but、or 等连接前后两个对等的部分,两个分句通常都用降调。例如：

John likes ↘ strawberries and ↘ apples.

I don't have a soccer ↘ ball, but my brother Alan ↘ does.

I couldn't really ↘ see or hear the ↘ guide.

We look ↘ similar but we're very ↘ different.

My favorite subject is ↘ art while her favorite subject is ↘ Chinese.

Lesson 11　Homework

Ⅰ. 跟读模仿以下句子发音,按要求提交模仿作业。

1. Go back to your seat!

2. What a small world!

Lesson 11　Intonation of different types of sentences　不同类型的句子的语调

3. Would you like coffee or tea?
4. Can you hand in your compositions today?
5. Will you take off your hat, please?
6. Are there many boys in your class?
7. How much time have you got?
8. Why are you not inviting Jane to your party?
9. Let's go to town tomorrow.
10. Can I have an apple or a banana?

Ⅱ. 跟读模仿下列对话,按要求提交模仿作业。

Sally: Ben! Why don't you have a rest and stop playing for a while? I've got homework.

Ben: What's up, Sally?

Sally: I've got English and Geography homework. And you're playing the guitar badly!

Ben: Well, it's my hobby and I have a good time when I practise. I love it.

Sally: Sure. But right now?

Ben: Well, yes! I'm practising now, then I can do my homework later.

Sally: Well, can you do your homework now, please? The same time as me? And then practise the guitar later?

Ben: Erm ... well, yes, why not? But help me with my Maths homework, OK?

Sally: Oh, all right!

Lesson 12 Review and examination of basic phonetic knowledge
基本语音复习检测

Ⅰ. Read the following phonetic symbols correctly. 正确识读下列音标。

1. [æ]   [ʊ]   [ð]   [g]   [uː]   [ts]   [t]   [h]   [ɪə]   [k]
2. [ə]   [eə]   [tr]   [aʊ]   [θ]   [ʃ]   [aɪ]   [eɪ]   [ʒ]   [d]
3. [iː]   [s]   [ɜː]   [ɒɪ]   [ŋ]   [ʊə]   [f]   [e]   [ɑː]   [r]
4. [b]   [aɪ]   [p]   [tʃ]   [z]   [ʌ]   [v]   [ɪ]   [dʒ]   [w]
5. [j]   [dr]   [m]   [eɪ]   [n]   [l]   [ɔː]   [ɒ]   [ʃ]   [θ]
6. [ʊ]   [iː]   [ə]   [k]   [h]   [g]   [ɪ]   [t]   [tr]   [ɔː]
7. [ʊə]   [θ]   [e]   [aʊ]   [eə]   [s]   [æ]   [əʊ]   [ɑː]   [d]
8. [ɔɪ]   [ɒ]   [ʃ]   [aɪ]   [p]   [ɜː]   [eɪ]   [v]   [dz]   [ð]
9. [ts]   [tʃ]   [ʌ]   [ɪə]   [l]   [b]   [m]   [uː]   [ŋ]   [j]
10. [w]   [ə]   [f]   [dr]   [z]   [æ]   [dʒ]   [ʊə]   [n]   [r]

Ⅱ. Read the following syllables correctly. 正确识读下列音标。

1. [iːt]   [ʌp]   [ɪə]   [ef]   [wʊd]   [ɪz]   [æm]   ['æpl]   [ɔːl]   [æt]
2. [eɪt]   [ɒɪl]   [ɪəz]   [ɔː(r)] [eə(r)] [ænd]   [eɪm] [əʊ'keɪ] [aʊt]
   [ænt]
3. [piː]   [tiː]   [kɔːl] [fuːd] [zuː]   [seɪl] [tʃɔː(r)] [triː] [ʃaɪ]

[tuː]

4. [bʊk]　[dæd]　[get]　[waɪ]　[səʊ]　[ˈzɪərəʊ]　[duː]　[drɔː]　[eg]
[dʒɒb]

5. [hɔːs]　[maɪn]　[nɔːθ]　[lʊk]　[raɪs]　[jɪə(r)]　[wiː]　[taʊn]
[faːm]　[tuːθ]

6. [ʃaʊt]　[dɒg]　[tʃes]　[ðiːz]　[pʊt]　[wɪð]　[dres]　[wɔːm]　[leg]
[puːl]

7. [ˈɪŋglɪʃ]　[ˈdʒækɪt]　[ˈjeləʊ]　[ˈpɜːpl]　[ˈsevn]　[ˈmɪdl]　[ˈwenzdeɪ]
[ˈjuːsfl]　[ˈtwentɪəθ]　[ˈhelθi]

8. [ˈriːəli]　[ˈtʃɪkɪn]　[ɪkˈskjuːz]　[ˈkʌzn]　[ˈiːmeɪl]　[ˈkɪtʃɪn]
[ˈmiːdɪəm]　[pəˈliːs]　[ˈmesɪdʒ]　[pliːz]

9. [ˈtelɪfəʊn]　[ˈfebruəri]　[ˈvedʒtəbl]　[ˈɪntrəstɪŋ]　[ˈdɪkʃənri]
[ɪˈreɪzə(r)]　[ˈfæməli]　[ˌɑːftəˈnuːn]　[kəmˈpjuːtə(r)]　[ˈlaɪbrəri]

10. [ˈfɪnɪʃ]　[ˈjuːʒuəli]　[ˈlæŋgwɪdʒ]　[ˈkrɪmɪnl]　[ˈfəʊtəʊ]　[ˈjuːnɪfɔːm]
[ˈvɒlɪbɔːl]　[ˈɪntrəstɪd]　[ˈkʌmpəni]　[ˈiːvnɪŋ]

Ⅲ. Read aloud the following sentences, paying attention to the liaison, loss of explosion, stressed words and intonation. 朗读下列句子,注意连读、失去爆破、重读单词、句子语调。

1. There is a hole in the door.
2. What's that in English?
3. How interesting!
4. Thank you for your help, Anna.
5. Don't leave the dirty dishes in the kitchen! (生气)
6. Come on, Jack! (催促)
7. You want to talk to her, don't you? (不确定)
8. They like pears but they don't like chicken.
9. How much are those yellow socks?

10. What are you doing?（质问）

11. Joe Brown has a very interesting job.

12. Are there any vegetables in the beef soup?

13. All of these birthday foods may be different, but the ideas are the same.

14. It was so much fun.

15. I think today's school trip was terrible.

16. Gina's books are everywhere—on the bed, on the sofa and under the chair.

17. Where's my schoolbag?

18. Hey, Helen, let's go!

19. I must find it.（一定要找到它）

20. I didn't like the trip at all.

Lesson 12　Homework

Ⅰ. 跟读模仿以下单词发音，按要求提交模仿作业。

food [fu:d]　　　　　drink [drɪŋk]　　　　　candy ['kændi]

fruit [fru:t]　　　　　vegetable ['vedʒtəbl]　　bean [bi:n]

beef [bi:f]　　　　　carrot ['kærət]　　　　　cola ['kəʊlə]

juice [dʒu:s]　　　　coffee ['kɒfi]　　　　　　soup [su:p]

children ['tʃɪldrən]　　noodle ['nu:dl]　　　　　ice cream [ˌaɪs'kri:m]

tooth [tu:θ]　　　　　tired [taɪəd]　　　　　　cheese [tʃi:z]

history ['hɪstri]　　　maths [mæθs]　　　　　because [bɪ'kɒz]

weekday ['wi:kdeɪ]　lesson ['lesən]　　　　　begin [bɪ'gɪn]

Lesson 12 Review and examination of basic phonetic knowledge
基本语音复习检测

Ⅱ. 跟读模仿下列对话,按要求提交模仿作业。

Jade: Mum, can I take judo lessons?

Mum: Judo? Really? What for?

Jade: Well ... it's good exercise, and some of my friends are learning judo, too.

Dad: I think it's a great idea.

Mum: Really? Judo for girls?

Jade: Mum!!

Dad: Yes, a friend of mine at work does judo. She loves it and she says it's very good for making her strong and keeping her healthy.

Jade: That's right, Dad. And maybe I can make some new friends, too.

Mum: Oh, well. OK.

Jade: Thanks, Mum! Thanks, Dad!

Dad: Jade! I think that's kung fu, not judo!

Lesson 13 Differences between British English and American English
英式英语和美式英语区分

Ⅰ. Differences in phonetic symbols between British English and American English and examples. 英式英语和美式英语在音标发音方面的区别及举例。

1. Pronunciation Table 发音表

   注:DJ 英式音标和 K.K. 美式音标都是 IPA 国际音标。

   以下是英式音标与美式音标的元音对照表：

Monophthongs and diphthongs

| IPA | | Example | IPA | | Example |
DJ	K.K.		DJ	K.K.	
iː	i	see[siː]/[si]	ɜː	ɝ	fur[fɜː(r)]/[fɝ]
ɪ	ɪ	sit[sɪt]/[sɪt]	ə	ə	ago[əˈgəʊ]/[əˈgo]
e	ɛ	ten[ten]/[tɛn]		ɚ	never[ˈnevə(r)]/[ˈnevɚ]
æ	æ	hat[hæt]/[hæt]	eɪ	e	page[peɪdʒ]/[pedʒ]
ɑː	ɑ	palm[pɑːm]/[pɑm]	əʊ	o	home[həʊm]/[hom]
	æ	ask[ɑːsk]/[æsk]	aɪ	aɪ	five[faɪv]/[faɪv]
ɒ	ɑ	watch[wɒtʃ]/[wɑtʃ]	aʊ	aʊ	now[naʊ]/[naʊ]
	ɔ	long[lɒŋ]/[lɔŋ]	ɔɪ	ɔɪ	join[dʒɔɪn]/[dʒɔɪn]
ɔː	ɔ	saw[sɔː]/[sɔ]	ɪə	ɪr	near[nɪə(r)]/[nɪr]
ʊ	ʊ	put[pʊt]/[pʊt]	eə	ɛr	hair[heə(r)]/[hɛr]
uː	u	too[tuː]/[tu]	ʊə	ʊr	tour[tʊə(r)]/[tʊr]
ʌ	ʌ	cup[kʌp]/[kʌp]			

Lesson 13 Differences between British English and American English
英式英语和美式英语区分

2. More examples 更多举例

注：每个单词两个音标，顺序为 DJ / K.K.；

没标注音标的单词，其元音音素的英式和美式发音相同。

1) Monophthong 单元音

a. [iː]—[i]　we [wiː]/[wi], sea [siː]/[si], he [hiː]/[hi], piece [piːs]/[pis], please [pliːz]/[pliz]

b. [ɪ]—[ɪ]　sit, if, pick, hit, pig

c. [e]—[ɛ]　bed [bed]/[bɛd], desk [desk]/[dɛsk], head [hed]/[hɛd], egg [eg]/[ɛg], set [set]/[sɛt]

d. [æ]—[æ]　bag, back, bank, map, apple.

e. [ɑː]—[ɑ]/[æ]　car [kɑː(r)]/[kar], after [ˈɑːftə(r)]/[ˈæftər], fast [fɑːst]/[fæst], class [klɑːs]/[klæs], plant [plɑːnt]/[plænt]

f. [ɒ]—[ɑ]/[ɔ]　hot [hɒt]/[hat], want [wɒnt]/[want; wɔnt], wrong [rɒŋ]/[rɔŋ], stop [stɒp]/[stap], long [lɒŋ]/[lɔŋ]

g. [ɔː]—[ɔ]　door [dɔː(r)]/[dɔr], more [mɔː]/[mɔr], sport [spɔːt]/[spɔrt], ball [bɔːl]/[bɔl], warm [wɔːm]/[wɔrm]

h. [uː]—[u]　who [huː]/[hu], blue [bluː]/[blu], soup [suːp]/[sup], boot [buːt]/[but], noon [nuːn]/[nun]

i. [ʊ]—[ʊ]　look, put, women, would, book

j. [ʌ]—[ʌ]　cup, come, lovely, other, bus

k. [ɜː]—[ɝ]　girl [gɜːl]/[gɝl], work [wɜːk]/[wɝk], first [fɜːst]/[fɝst], nurse [nɜːs]/[nɝs], earth [ɜːθ]/[ɝθ]

l. [ə]—[ə]/[ɚ]　ago, polite, forget [fəˈget]/[fɚˈgɛt], dollar [ˈdɒlə(r)]/[ˈdalɚ], doctor [ˈdɒktə(r)]/[ˈdaktɚ]

2) Diphthong 双元音

a. [eɪ]—[e]　cake [keɪk]/[kek], they [ðeɪ]/[ðe], play [pleɪ]/[ple], eight [eɪt]/[et], great [greɪt]/[gret]

b. [aɪ]—[aɪ]　bike, drive, height, light, try

c. [əʊ]—[o] phone [fəʊn]/[fon], cold [kəʊld]/[kold], boat [bəʊt]/[bot], nose [nəʊz]/[noz], grow [grəʊ]/[gro]

d. [aʊ]—[aʊ] house, town, how, blouse, mouth

e. [ɔɪ]—[ɔɪ] boy, oil, roil, soil, toy

f. [ɪə]—[ɪr] dear [dɪə(r)]/[dɪr], deer [dɪə(r)]/[dɪr], here [hɪə(r)]/[hɪr], ear [ɪə(r)]/[ɪr], year [jɪə(r)]/[jɪr]

g. [eə]—[ɛr] pear [peə(r)]/[pɛr], care [keə(r)]/[kɛr], there [ðeə(r)]/[ðɛr], air [eə(r)]/[ɛr], share [ʃeə(r)]/[ʃɛr]

h. [ʊə]—[ʊr] poor [pʊə(r)]/[pʊr], sure [ʃʊə(r)]/[ʃʊr]

II. Differences in pronunciation and intonation between British English and American English and examples. 英式英语和美式英语在语音语调方面的区别及举例。

1. Differences in vowels 元音差别

1) 字母 a 在[s][f][m][n][θ][ð][l]等之前,英式英语发音为[ɑː],而在美式英语中则为[æ],例如:ask, past, fast, class, after, dance, path, half。

但是,当字母 a 在[p][b][t][d][k][g]等之后时,英语和美语都发作[æ],例如:pad, bag, dad, cat, carrot, gap。

2) 英式英语中的[ɔː]和[ɒ],相应的在美语中发作[ɔ]和[a]。当然,美语在发这两个音时开口度稍大一些。

a. 在字母组合 au, al, aul 中,例如:fault, halt, daughter, hall。

b. 在[p][b][t][d][k][g]等音之前,例如:dog, hot, got, pop, Bob。

3) -ile 在美语中发作[l][əl],而在英语中一般发作[aɪl],例如:fragile, missile, mobile。

4) 在-ary, -ery, -ory 中,字母 a,e,o 在英语中一般发作[ə]音,而美语中一般省略,例如:library, bakery, factory, history。

5) 形存实亡的[ʌ]音。同[ɪ]音一样,英式和美式英语的[ʌ]音标虽然拼写一

Lesson 13　Differences between British English and American English
英式英语和美式英语区分

致,但实际的运用却是不尽相同的。美语里倾向于把英音中的[ʌ]音多半发成[ə]音,如 hurry [ˈhʌri]/ [ˈhəri]。

2. Differences in consonants 辅音差别

1) 字母 t 的发音

在没有重读且处于两个元音音素之间的时候,美语中字母 t 的发音近于[d],例如:matter, waiter, city, waiting。

注意:如果处于重读音节中或在非重读音节中的清辅音之后,或者处在一个音节的最后,字母 t 不管是在英语中还是在美语中都发作[t],例如:obtain, return, master。

2) [j]的发音

在英语中一般保留,而在美语中一般消失。在[t] [d] [n] [θ] [l] [s]之后,字母及字母组合 u, ew, eu 在英语中一般发作[juː],而在美语中发作[uː],例如:tube [tjuːb]/[tuːb], duty [ˈdjuːti]/[ˈduːti], new [njuː]/[nuː], neutral [ˈnjuːtrəl]/[ˈnuːtrəl]。

注意:在[h] [m] [b] [k] [f] [v]之后,字母及字母组合 u, eu 和 ew 不管是在英语还是在美语中都发作[juː],例如:huge [hjuːdʒ]/[hjuːdʒ], music [ˈmjuːzɪk]/[ˈmjuːzɪk], feudal [ˈfjuːdl]/[ˈfjuːdl], few [fjuː]/[fjuː]。

3) 字母 r

在字母组合 ar, er, ur, ir, or, ear, eer, air, oor, ore, our, ere, are 等中,在美语中会发作[r],而在英语中不发音,例如:hear, person, park, river, north。

注意:如果[r]在元音之前,不管是在美语中还是在英语中都要发音,例如:read, race, remember, rain, real。

3. The sentence stress and intonation 句子的重音和语调

1) 英式英语的发音比较讲究抑扬顿挫,起伏感比较强,更具有音乐性,其语调从最高位到最低位之间音域较宽广,且其最高音位一般在句首,后面部分的语调逐渐下降。而美式英语听起来比较平直,变化较小,调域变化较少,直至句尾才稍有变化。

2) 美语与英语在重音上差异悬殊,表现在两个方面:一个是单词的重音,另一个是句子的重音。前者属个别现象,后者属普遍现象。

a. 先谈单词的重音差异,英国人习惯于将单词重音放在第一个音节上,而美国人则放在第二个音节上,如 ballet [ˈbæleɪ]/[bæˈleɪ], cafe [ˈkæfeɪ]/[kæˈfeɪ]。不过有时则又要反过来说,即英国人重读第二个音节,美国人重读第一个音节,典型的如 research [rɪˈsɜːtʃ]/[ˈriːsɜːrtʃ]。另外,还包括一些以 ham、wich、cester 等结尾的地名发音差异。在这一点上,我们并没有什么太多的规律可遵循,建议在学习单词时要特别注意一下重音的英美音不同的标注。

b. 句子重音差异:美语在简化原则的指导下,将句子重音压缩成一到两个,所重读的也就是说话人想强调的内容,句子说得就如同一个单词,这就是著名的语言连锁现象。重音位要读得慢些清楚些,非重音位要通过连读爆破尤其是弱化一气呵成。而英音,则是重音散乱,一个句子的重音通常集中在实词、特殊疑问词、感叹词、指示代词及人称代词等上面。我们因此普遍有一种感觉,美语发音含糊不清,而英音口齿清楚。

4．Examples 举例

1) What sports can you play?

2) I eat breakfast at nine.

3) He works at a radio station.

4) What time do you usually get up?

5) Do you want the large size or the small size?

Lesson 13　Homework

Ⅰ．跟读模仿下列对话,按要求提交模仿作业。

Mum: Harry! It's time for dinner.

Mum: Come on, Harry. Dinner's ready.

Lesson 13 Differences between British English and American English
英式英语和美式英语区分

Harry: Just a minute, Mum. I'm finishing something.

Mum: Harry, it's dinnertime. Come and eat. We're having dinner!

Harry: OK, Mum.

Mum: You're always on your phone or playing games.

Harry: No, not games, Mum. Puzzles. I'm doing a crossword.

Mum: A crossword? Oh, I hate crosswords. They're too difficult.

Harry: I love them. They're great exercise for my brain.

Mum: Are they? Well, OK. You know, you have to look after your brain, right?

Harry: That's right. Just like you look after me, Mum.

Lesson 14　Sentence imitation 句子模仿

Ⅰ. Sentence imitation 句子模仿

1. 普通陈述句

    I am thirty years ↘old.

2. 陈述疑问句

    I beg your ↗ pardon?

3. 一般疑问句

    Is this your ↗ pencil?

4. 一般疑问句读降调表示批评或指责

    Is there anything you want to ↘say?

5. 特殊疑问句

    What did you do last ↘ weekend?

    How much is↗ it?（表示温和的批评，如嫌弃价格太高）

6. 表示命令的祈使句

    Be ↘quiet.

7. 感叹句

    What a ↘pity!

8. 选择疑问句

    Do you like↗chicken, ↗pork or ↘ fish?

9. 反意疑问句

    Let's go to the ↘party together, ↗shall we?

10. 句首的状语

    A moment↗later, she arrived at ↘ school.

11. 并列句或并列成分

He sat down↗ by my side,↗ took out a piece of paper and↘ gave it to me.

Ⅱ. Practice 练习

1. I see.
2. Happy birthday!
3. Are you Helen?
4. It's cold, isn't it?
5. What should I do?
6. Let's see the pandas.
7. Did you ride a horse?
8. That's not very nice, is it?
9. Can their dream come true?
10. We are meeting at seven, right?
11. Can I take a message for him?
12. They are my favourite animals.
13. Can't we make jokes about friends?
14. Why do you want to see them, Lucy?
15. How is your summer vacation going?
16. I think you should lie down and rest.
17. How did Lisa feel when she saw the snake?
18. Are there any vegetables in the beef noodles?
19. It doesn't matter whether you are rich or famous or not.
20. The teacher says it is useful, but I think it is difficult.
21. What about burgers, vegetable salad, and some fruit?
22. As soon as we arrive, we're going on a tour of the city.
23. She is of medium height, and she has long straight hair.

24. The weather here is cool and cloudy, just right for walking.

25. If your head and neck still hurt tomorrow, then go to a doctor.

26. Why don't I come around to your place this afternoon after school?

27. My dad told me later that snakes don't have ears but they can feel things moving.

28. One large bowl of beef soup, one *gongbao* chicken, and one *mapo* tofu with rice.

29. The room was really dark and it was difficult to take photos, so I did not take any.

30. In some places, Chinese people also eat eggs on their birthday, because they are a symbol of life and good luck.

Lesson 14   Homework

Ⅰ. 跟读模仿以下句子发音,按要求提交模仿作业。

1. Reading aloud / is very important / for beginners.
2. Early to bed / and early to rise / makes a man / healthy, happy, and wise.
3. Jane, / who's a brilliant swimmer, / represented Britain / at the Olympic Games.
4. After he took his bath, / he dressed in a hurry, / ran to catch the bus, / and got to his appointment / before it was too late.
5. By the time he arrived / he was completely exhausted.

Ⅱ. 跟读模仿下列对话,按要求提交模仿作业。

Ryan: All right, Mum?

Lesson 14 Sentence imitation 句子模仿

Mum: No, not really. Ryan, I really need you to help me.

Ryan: Sorry, Mum? What did you say?

Mum: I said I need some help, Ryan. There are so many things to do in this house.

Ryan: Like what?

Mum: Well, this washing up, for a start. Look at all this! It's terrible. So, can you do it for me before you go out, please?

Ryan: No chance, Mum! I'm leaving soon and I've got lots of things to do. I'm really busy, you know.

Mum: What do you mean?

Ryan: Well, homework and stuff. You know.

Mum: OK. Never mind. You don't have to help me. But I have to leave soon. I have a meeting with a new client. I mustn't be late.

Ryan: Oh, OK. Sorry, Mum. Don't worry. I can do it. Leave it all to me, OK?

Mum: Are you sure?

Ryan: Absolutely. You go now and leave everything to me.

Mum: OK, thanks Ryan. You're a good boy! Bye!

Ryan: OK, well it is a lot of washing up, and perhaps I should clean the kitchen, too. But the game starts right now and there's no TV in here. Hmm. Problem. Some creative thinking is needed. Well, it's easy of course. Get my phone. Do live streaming of the game. Put the phone next to the sink. And great! Off we go. And the game's starting. Come on, United. Argh, no! That's my new phone!

Lesson 15　Dialogue imitation 对话模仿

Ⅰ. Listen and imitate 听录音,模仿下列对话

A

Sally: Good morning, Jane.

Jane: Good morning, Sally.

Sally: Oh, Jane, this is my sister Kate. Kate, this is my friend Jane.

Kate: Nice to meet you, Jane.

Jane: Nice to meet you, too. Are those your parents?

Kate: Yes, they are.

Jane: And who's he?

Sally: He's my brother, Paul.

Jane: Oh, I see. Well, have a good day!

Sally/Kate: Thanks! You, too. Bye!

B

Mom: Come on, Jack!

Jack: Oh, no! Where's my bag?

Mom: Hmm... is it on your desk?

Jack: No. And it's not under the chair.

Mom: Oh! It's on the sofa.

Jack: Thank you, Mum. Er... where's the map?

Mom: I think it's in your grandparents' room.

Jack: Yes, it's on their bed! And my hat?

Mom: It's on your head!

Jack: Oh, yeah! Haha!

C

Mike: Hi, Tony. Are you going to the movie tonight?

Tony: Yes. We're meeting at seven, right?

Mike: Yeah, but I may be a little late. My friend David is going, too. Just meet him in front of the cinema first.

Tony: Oh, but I don't know him. What does he look like?

Mike: Well, he has brown hair and wears glasses.

Tony: OK. Is he tall or short?

Mike: He isn't tall or short. He is of medium height.

Tony: OK, sure. See you later then.

D

Woman: Can I help you?

Mary: Yes, please. I need a sweater for school.

Woman: OK. What color do you want?

Mary: Blue.

Woman: How about this one?

Mary: It looks nice. How much is it?

Woman: Nine dollars.

Mary: I'll take it. How much are those yellow socks?

Woman: Two dollars for one pair and three dollars for two pairs.

Mary: Great! I'll take two pairs.

Woman: Here you are.

Mary: Thank you.

Woman: You're welcome.

E

Frank: Hi, Bob. How's your day?

Bob: It's OK. I like Monday because I have P. E. and history. They're my favorite subjects.

Frank: Who's your P. E. teacher?

Bob: Mr. Hu. He always plays games with us.

Frank: That's great! But why do you like history? It's boring.

Bob: Oh, I think history is interesting. What's your favorite day?

Frank: Friday.

Bob: Why?

Frank: Because the next day is Saturday!

Bob: Haha! That's for sure. I like Friday, too.

Lesson 15   Homework

Ⅰ. 跟读模仿下列对话,按要求提交模仿作业。

James: Excuse me. Can we get our ball, please?

Alice: Yes, of course.

James: Oh, what a lovely garden!

Alice: Thank you. That's a nice thing to say. Do you like gardening, then?

James: Well, not really. I don't know much about flowers and things. But my sister loves them, don't you, Gill?

Gill: That's right. And your flowers really look wonderful. I love your roses.

Alice: Thank you again. I do it all myself, you know. My husband helped me before, but he can't walk very well now, so I have to do it all.

It's a lot of work. I get very, very tired.

Gill: Well, we can help you—can't we, James?

James: We're in the middle of a game and I'm winning! Maybe another day.

Gill: We can finish our game later, James. What would you like us to do?

Alice: What nice people you are! Well, perhaps you can help me move the table and chairs under that tree. They're in the sun at the moment and it's very hot. But first, I just need to make a phone call and a cup of tea. I'll be back in a minute.

James: No problem. We're fine here. OK. Let's move the table first. We can do that together. Then the chairs.

Moments later...

Alice: Oh, that's fantastic. Well done! Look, let me give you some money for some ice cream or chocolate, to say thank you.

Gill: No, please. We're happy to help. Come on, James. Bye!

James: How nice! She wanted to give us some money!

Gill: I know. And I feel so good now. I don't want ice cream, or chocolate, either. Her smile was enough.

James: That's right. But let's get some ice cream anyway!

Lesson 16　Passage imitation 语篇模仿

Ⅰ. Listen and imitate. 听录音,模仿下列语篇。

Birthday food around the world

What would people like to eat on their birthday? The answer would be different in different countries.

In many countries, people have birthday cakes with candles. The number of candles is the person's age. The birthday person must make a wish and blow out the candles. If he or she blows out all the candles in one go, the wish will come true. In the UK, people sometimes put a candy in a birthday cake. The child with the candy is lucky.

In China, it is getting popular to have cake on your birthday. But many people still eat very long noodles for their birthday. They never cut up the noodles because the long noodles are a symbol of long life. In some places, Chinese people also eat eggs on their birthday. They are a symbol of life and good luck.

All of these birthday foods may be different, but the ideas are the same. They bring good luck to the birthday person.

Lesson 16　Homework

Ⅰ. 跟读模仿以下语篇发音,按要求提交模仿作业。

Our holiday castle

　　We're still in Ireland. We arrived in Dublin four days ago. My sister and I liked it a lot — it was great — we weren't bored at all! Then yesterday, after lunch, Dad hired a car and we travelled to the west of Ireland. It didn't take very long, just about two and a half hours, but that was a bit boring. After two hours, Dad turned round to us and said, "We've got a surprise for you. Tonight our hotel is a castle! How exciting is that?" A joke, right? Wrong! We didn't think he was serious, but he was!

　　At the end of the journey, we stopped outside a real castle. A nice lady welcomed us and started to show us around. What an amazing place! Can you believe that we walked up fifty stone steps to get to the living room?

　　The castle is over 600 years old, but it had everything we needed. There was a bedroom for our parents and we each had a bedroom, too. But I didn't sleep very well last night — I was so excited to be in a real castle!

　　This morning we had breakfast and then we climbed up to the top of the castle. We were amazed at the beautiful countryside around us. Then it started to rain and there was a fantastic rainbow — I love rainbows!

　　The place was so great, and we didn't want to leave. This afternoon we want to go to Limerick, so we're packing our bags again! Can it be as good as a castle? Let's see.

附表1 英语国际音标四线三格书写规范

长元音	[iː]	[uː]	[ɜː]	[ɔː]	[ɑː]			
短元音	[ɪ]	[ʊ]	[ə]	[ɒ]	[e]	[æ]	[ʌ]	
双元音	[ɪə]	[ɔɪ]	[aɪ]	[ɪə]	[ʊə]	[eə]	[əʊ]	[aʊ]
清辅音	[p]	[t]	[k]	[f]	[ʃ]	[s]	[θ]	
浊辅音	[b]	[d]	[g]	[v]	[ʒ]	[z]	[ð]	
清辅音	[ts]	[tʃ]	[tr]	[h]				
浊辅音	[dz]	[dʒ]	[dr]	[r]				
鼻音	[m]	[n]	[ŋ]					
半元音	[j]	[w]						
舌侧音	[l]	含糊音	[ɫ]					

附表2　26个英文字母的书写及发音

Alphabet (Handwriting)						
Aa	Bb	Cc	Dd	Ee	Ff	Gg
[eɪ]	[biː]	[siː]	[diː]	[iː]	[ef]	[dʒiː]
Hh	Ii	Jj	Kk	Ll	Mm	Nn
[eɪtʃ]	[aɪ]	[dʒeɪ]	[keɪ]	[el]	[em]	[en]
Oo	Pp	Qq	Rr	Ss	Tt	
[əʊ]	[piː]	[kjuː]	[ɑː]	[es]	[tiː]	
Uu	Vv	Ww	Xx	Yy	Zz	
[juː]	[viː]	[ˈdʌblju:]	[eks]	[waɪ]	[ziː][zed]	

附录3 七年级新目标上册英语诵读小文

一、向别人介绍自己或家人

1. 给朋友写信,介绍自己和自己的家人。

Dear Mary,

　　I'm David. I am from England. I want to tell you about my family. Four people are in my family. They are my mother, my father, my sister and me.

　　I am a student in No. 1 Middle School. My father is an English teacher. He likes fishing very much. My mother is a doctor. She likes cooking. Chicken is her favorite food. My sister Julia and I are in the same school. We don't like eating vegetables. But my parents tell us to eat more vegetables. They are good for our health.

　　Look! We have a happy family! Can you write and tell me about you and your family?

Yours,
David

2. 假如你是张平,明天的英语课上老师要求你们介绍自己和家庭成员的年龄以及生日情况。请你根据自己的实际情况写一篇文章。

　　Hello, boys and girls. I am Zhang Ping. My English name is Alice. I'm from Zhengzhou and I am 13 years old now. I am a student in a middle school. My telephone number is 65587172. My birthday is on November 26th. Four people are in my family. They are my parents, my brother and me. My parents are teachers. They are very nice to their students. My father is 39 and his birthday is on May 17th. My mother is 37 and her birthday is on August 22nd.

My brother is a student, too. He is only nine years old. His birthday is on July 1st.

I love my family because they are very good to me. That's all. Thanks!

二、失物招领类

Lost:

I lost a pencil box in Classroom 8D this morning. It's blue and white. What's in it? A set of keys, two pens and a ruler are in it. I must find my pencil box. Please call me at 010-88967896. And you can e-mail me at mike@gmail.com. Thank you.

Mike

Found:

I found a schoolbag in the school library this afternoon. It's red. Two English books, a dictionary and a blue pencil box are in it. Is this your schoolbag? My phone number is 021-78996688. And you can e-mail me at sandy@gmail.com.

Sandy

三、描述房间

Hello, this is my room. It's nice and tidy. You can see a bed, a desk, a sofa and a bookcase in it. My quilt and jacket are on the bed. A black computer is on my desk. Next to my desk is the brown sofa. My schoolbag is on the sofa. And some books are in the bookcase. What's that under the bed? It's my baseball. I like my room very much!

四、商品促销广告

假如你是秦雪,你妈妈在街上开了一家名为 Fashion Clothes Store 的服装店,受到了很多外国朋友的青睐。最近店里要组织一次促销活动,请你根据表格内容,写一则促销广告,以便更多人光顾。

(表格显示毛衣各种颜色都有,80元一件;裤子有黑、白、红三色,60元一条,100元两条;运动鞋的颜色有黑、白色,70元一双。)

Welcome to our clothes store. We are at a great sale now. Do you need sweaters? We have sweaters in all colors. How much are they? Only 80 *yuan*. And we have nice trousers in black, white and red. They are only 60 *yuan* for a pair and 100 *yuan* for two pairs. Do you like sports shoes? They are at a very good price, too. We have black and white shoes. You can buy one pair for only 70 *yuan*. Anybody can afford our prices!

Come to Fashion Clothes Store and have a look now!

五、健康的生活方式(饮食+运动)

1. 最近,某英语杂志社举办题目为"Healthy lifestyle(生活方式)"的征文大赛。假如你是某中学七年级学生,请你结合自己认为健康的生活方式写一篇短文,给该杂志社投稿。

Nowadays, students like to eat hamburgers, but they don't like to eat vegetables. They like to play computer games, but they don't like to play sports.

I think students need to eat healthier food like fruit and vegetables. They also need to do sports. It's really relaxing to play sports with friends after school. I think doing sports can help them to be healthy.

2. 你的朋友李华不喜欢体育运动,也不爱吃水果和蔬菜。作为好朋友,请你快给她一些好的建议吧。

Dear Li Hua,

It is important to keep healthy. I have some advice for you.

I think you should often play sports. You can run after school on the playground every day. You can also go swimming or play basketball with friends on weekends. I think it is relaxing and good for you to play sports. Why don't you eat vegetables and fruit a lot? They are delicious and good for your health. You should eat well and have very good eating habits. For breakfast, you can have eggs, bread and milk. For lunch, you can have rice, chicken and carrots. And for dinner, you'd better have vegetable salad.

Have a try! And you can be healthy and strong.

Yours,
Lily

六、活动邀请/通知类

Dear friends,

I am very glad to invite you to my birthday party. It is my thirteenth birthday party. The party is on Saturday afternoon at my home. It is from 3:00 to 5:00. You can have some healthy food and play interesting games at the party. I hope you can have a good time!

Lily

七、校园生活类

1. 假如你是李华,就读于育地国际中学七年级。最近你的美国笔友Tony告诉你他要来你学校交流学习,他想了解你们学校的一些情况。请你给他回一封电子邮件,介绍你学校的情况。

学校相关情况:课程安排＋在校运动情况＋学校组织的活动。

Hi Tony,

I am happy you'll come to China and study at my school. I'll tell you something about it. I have a colorful school life. I have six classes a day—four in the morning and two in the afternoon. Our first class is at 8:00 in the morning and the last one is at 3:10 in the afternoon. I have eleven subjects this term. Of all the subjects, I like English best. It is easy and it's really useful.

At school, I can play sports with my classmates. We often play volleyball and have great fun. We have many school activities, like the soccer game, the art festival, the English party and the school trip. I think they are very interesting.

I hope you can come to our school. See you soon.

Yours,

Li Hua

2. 假如你是李海，你的笔友 Jim 来信询问你的学校生活，请根据表格内容给他写一封回信。（表格包含上课情况、课后活动、最喜欢的课及原因、最不喜欢的课及原因）

Dear Jim,

Thanks for your letter. Do you want to know about my school life?

Well, I usually have four classes from 8:00 to 11:30 in the morning and two classes from 2:30 to 4:00 in the afternoon. I often play ping-pong or sing songs after class. English and P. E. are my favorite subjects, because they are easy and interesting. But I don't like geography, because it is difficult.

What is your school life like? Write and tell me about it!

Yours,

Li Hai

3. 请以"My favorite subject"为题，写一篇短文。

My favorite subject

My favorite subject is English. English is very useful in the world. We often meet foreigners in public places. We can talk to them easily in English. My English teacher is kind and friendly, so it makes me like English better. I like reading English stories and listening to English songs. I can learn a lot about English culture from them. I often watch English news on TV. So I know what is going on around the world. I have a lot of fun learning English.

In a word, I love English very much. I will study hard and try to learn English well.

八、介绍朋友类

1. 请以"My best friend"为题，写一篇小作文。

My best friend

My best friend is Daniel. He is 13 years old. He is short and he wears a pair of glasses. He often wears a purple T-shirt and a pair of grey trousers. He looks very cool.

Daniel has a healthy lifestyle. He often exercises. He seldom has hamburgers and coke because he thinks they are bad for his health. He is interested in drawing. What's more, he likes playing computer games. There is a shopping mall near his home. He often goes shopping there. And he thinks it is a good place to have fun.

This is my best friend Daniel. I think we will be friends forever.

2. 假如李华是你的好朋友，请写一篇短文，介绍她的基本情况。（内容包含年龄、生日、饮食习惯、最喜欢的科目以及原因、活动安排）

Li Hua is my friend. She is 12 years old. Her birthday is on July 3rd. She gets up at 6:30 and then she has an egg and a glass of milk for breakfast. She goes to school at 7:30. Her classes begin at 8:00. She has four classes in the morning and two classes in the afternoon. Her favorite subject is English, because it is interesting. She has lunch at school. Her classes finish at 5:00. After that, she often plays basketball with her classmates. She gets home at 7:00. After supper, she often has some fruit and does her homework.

附录4 《简明语音教程》使用参考手册

课序	完成内容	需完成学习目标或任务	课时建议
附表1	英语国际音标四线三格书写规范	书面作业;建议随课程进行书写练习	
Lesson 1	Monophthongs 单元音	能正确拼读单元音(检查形式可多样);能书写所有的单元音音标;模仿背诵附录中的诵读小文一篇。	2
Lesson 2	Diphthongs 双元音	能正确拼读双元音(检查形式可多样);能书写所有的双元音音标;模仿背诵附录中的诵读小文一篇。	1
Lesson 3	Consonants Ⅰ 辅音(一)	能正确拼读本课内辅音(检查形式可多样);能书写本课辅音音标;模仿背诵附录中的诵读小文一篇。	1~2
Lesson 4	Consonants Ⅱ 辅音(二)	能正确拼读本课内辅音(检查形式可多样);能书写本课辅音音标;模仿背诵附录中的诵读小文一篇。	2
Lesson 5	Mixed practice of vowels and consonants 元音辅音混合练习	形式多样地检查学生对元音辅音的掌握情况;模仿背诵附录中的诵读小文一篇。	1
Lesson 6	Practice of monosyllables 单音节拼读练习	能够正确拼读单音节的单词(检查形式可多样);模仿背诵附录中的诵读小文一篇。	1
Lesson 7	Practice of disyllables 双音节拼读练习	能够总结音节划分规则并熟记;模仿背诵附录中的诵读小文一篇。	1
Lesson 8	Practice of polysyllables 多音节拼读练习	能够正确划分和拼读多音节单词;模仿背诵附录中的诵读小文一篇。	1
Lesson 9	Mixed practice of monosyllables, disyllables and polysyllables 单音节、双音节、多音节混合拼读练习	能够完成单音节、双音节、多音节混合拼读练习;模仿背诵附录中的诵读小文一篇。	1

续表

课序	完成内容	需完成学习目标或任务	课时建议
Lesson 10	Stress, liaison and loss of plosion 重读、连读、失去爆破	熟记重读、弱读、连读和失去爆破常见规则和常见单词读音；反复练习课本上的例句；模仿背诵附录中的诵读小文一篇。	2
Lesson 11	Intonation of different types of sentences 不同类型的句子的语调	熟记升调和降调的常见规则；在句子中练习升调和降调；模仿背诵附录中的诵读小文一篇。	2
Lesson 12	Review and examination of basic phonetic knowledge 基本语音复习检测	能够背默48个国际音标；能够根据音标拼读单词，看单词尝试拼读；朗读句子，并注意连读、失去爆破和语调等语音现象。	1
Lesson 13	Differences between British English and American English 英式英语和美式英语区分	能够欣赏英音和美音录音片段，识别英音或美音；学生根据自身情况确定自己适合发英音还是美音。	1
Lesson 14	Sentence imitation 句子模仿	跟读句子，模仿录音中的语音语调和感情。	1
Lesson 15	Dialogue imitation 对话模仿	跟读对话，模仿录音中的语音语调和感情，结对练习。	1
Lesson 16	Passage imitation 语篇模仿	跟读并尝试背诵语篇，模仿录音中的语音语调和感情。	1
附表 2	26个英文字母的书写及发音	准确书写26个字母的大小写（笔顺，占格）；准确读出26个字母；能写出26个字母的音标。	2
附录 3	七年级新目标上册英语诵读小文	作为语音学习期间的模仿背诵篇章。	